THIS ONE WILL HURT YOU

21st CENTURY ESSAYS
David Lazar and Patrick Madden, Series Editors

THIS ONE
WILL
HURT YOU

PAUL CRENSHAW

MAD CREEK BOOKS, AN IMPRINT OF
THE OHIO STATE UNIVERSITY PRESS
COLUMBUS

Library of Congress Cataloging-in-Publication Data
Names: Crenshaw, Paul, 1972– author.
Title: This one will hurt you / Paul Crenshaw.
Other titles: 21st century essays.
Description: Columbus : Mad Creek Books, an imprint of The Ohio State
    University Press, [2019] | Series: 21st century essays
Identifiers: LCCN 2018044821 | ISBN 9780814255216 (pbk. ; alk. paper) |
    ISBN 0814255213 (pbk. ; alk. paper)
Subjects: LCSH: American essays—21st century.
Classification: LCC PS3603.R458 A6 2019 | DDC 814/.6—dc23

LC record available at https://lccn.loc.gov/2018044821

Cover design by Christian Fuenfhausen
Text design by Juliet Williams
Type set in Adobe Sabon

♾ The paper used in this publication meets the minimum requirements of the
American National Standard for Information Sciences—Permanence of Paper
for Printed Library Materials. ANSI Z39.48-1992.

CONTENTS

AFTER THE ICE

When I was seventeen an ice storm moved through my hometown in Arkansas and coated the roads and trees with a thin layer of ice. I remember the ice only because later that morning I would receive a phone call that my nephew Keith, my stepsister's son, was in the hospital. There were few details, just that he was hurt in some way and it looked serious, and driving there, the day was so bright it hurt the muscles behind my eyes. Ice covered the fields where cows searched for grass, their breath fanning the air before them. On top of telephone poles hawks sat waiting, sharp eyes scanning the fields for movement. The few cars on the road drove slowly, fearing the ice, though by that time it was melting, and small streams ran across the road, the water turned brown and dirty from the salt and cinders the county road crews had dumped the night before.

At the hospital, my family gathered in the hall outside the emergency room. Every few minutes the door opened and a nurse came out, and when the door opened we could see my nephew laid out on the operating table, tubes down his throat, his pajamas open and his small chest, thin and frail as a bird's, failing to rise and fall. He was eighteen months old.

In a few hours he would be pronounced dead, and not long after that one of the nurses on duty would call the police to report that this was not an accident. There were bruises on his neck and shoulders, and before night fell again Keith's stepfather was under investigation for murder.

I have scans of the old newspaper articles saved on my computer now. My mother, at my request, found old microfilm reels at the library and emailed them to me. I read them sometimes, late at night, when my daughters are asleep, though when they first arrived in my inbox, it took me months to open them.

The first one is dated February 8, and is titled "Boy's Death Investigated." According to the article, the un-named boy died of "severe head injuries," and after his death his body was sent to the state medical examiner in Little Rock. The Logan County Sheriff stated that police were waiting on an autopsy, but they suspected the boy's death was related to child abuse.

The next article is six months later. After three days of trial, and a jury deliberation of less than two hours, the stepfather was convicted of first degree murder. In his testimony, he said that his stepson had wandered outside while he was on the phone. In the courtroom he was clean-shaven, his hair cut short, and he wore a long-sleeve blue shirt with a dark blue tie. His hands moved as he talked, and his eyes roamed about the courtroom, not landing on anyone. When he hung up the phone, he saw the boy outside, by the woodpile. He lay on his back, the stepfather said. He was not moving.

At the hospital, the nurses first noticed, and later the medical examiner confirmed, four small bruises on Keith's forehead. There were large pictures set up on exhibit stands in the courtroom, and the medical examiner pointed to each one with a pointer. He made a circling motion around the four bruises, spaced apart like knuckles. There were also deep bruises on Keith's neck. In the courtroom the picture sat next to another picture of my nephew in overalls, holding a stuffed tiger. He was smiling then, laughing at whatever silly toy the cameraman was holding up. He had only a few teeth in the picture, and his blonde hair was combed so fine you could hardly see it, like the way a baby's hair will disappear in the bathtub. As he was shaken, his brain crashed around inside his skull. The blood vessels feeding his brain were torn. Blood pooled within his skull, creating pressure. His brain swelled. At some point he lost consciousness. He was not breathing when he arrived at the hospital. In the hours he lay on the emergency room table, he did not breathe on his own. In the parking lot my stepbrother lit one cigarette from the butt of another. In the hallway outside the room, we all waited, impotent and raging. In the big corner mirrors the nurses came and went.

I reconstruct the physical injuries from newspaper reports and courtroom testimony to cement the crime in my head. Years later I sometimes feel forgiveness creeping in, so I list in my head the bruises and choke marks. I think about time, how long this must have gone on, and some strange feeling builds up in me, though it is not sadness, or anger. Perhaps it is despair. But in the years since, most of the sadness has fled, and what remains exists only on an intellectual level. I have no visceral reaction, and I am surprised to find no emotion, only a place where that emotion used to be. I'd like to say sadness has replaced it, but in the time that has passed what is left is a feeling deeper than sadness. But it is less painful. It is like trees in November, or birdsong before first light; something intangible, full of memory and heartache: a child's clean smell, a faint memory of your mother, a daughter's first steps.

If my nephew had lived he might have had physical and learning disabilities, seizures, behavioral disorders, cerebral palsy, and speech and hearing impairment. He might not have walked again, or spoken. He might not have ever learned his name, or his mother's birthday. He might not have remembered what happened to him, and for some reason I cannot explain, though I am ashamed to say it, this seems unbearable to me—that he might have smiled when his stepfather came into the room, or reached up his arms for his stepfather to pick him up, or laid his head on his stepfather's chest late at night on the couch, the TV the only light in the room, changing from light to dark.

The last article is the shortest of all. It recounts the sentencing hearing, in which the stepfather was sentenced to life in prison. When the sentence was given, his attorney put a hand on his shoulder. He was not wearing a tie this time. He was in jailhouse orange sweats, with black numbers stenciled on them, and his hands were handcuffed in front of him. It is an image I will remember for a very long time, held up against the one of my nephew with tubes down his throat, but the two of them do not cancel one another out, just as recounting the newspaper articles does not cancel out the story inside my head.

The funeral was in a church I had never been to before. It exists now in a cloistral space—nothing before it or after it. It is an isolated incident, faint at the edges of memory. There was an easel set up with a picture of Keith on it, the same picture of overalls and a stuffed tiger that would sit in the courtroom when the trial started. The casket was closed. I suspect it would have been too hard any other way. I sat in a balcony of the church with my grandmother. I suspect it was a strategic positioning, that from the distance of the balcony her failing eyes could not make out the picture, the flowers, the casket.

Two police officers sat near the stepfather, their uniforms crisply ironed. He sat near the front of the church and stared straight ahead. From the balcony I studied his profile—red hair that reached to the nape of his neck, a mustache not trimmed well. His face was red, pale blotch that crept higher up his neck and side of his face, and his jaw worked as the service went on.

During the service my eyes wandered from the tiger to the stepfather to the state troopers, then made the loop again and again. My grandmother moaned beside me, a noise she did not know she was making, just as she didn't know what had happened, or why, and I realized in a strange moment of clarity, one that announced my emergence into adulthood, that we would never understand, that for the rest of our lives when any of this was mentioned, we would shake our heads sadly and stare at the floor until the moment passed.

After the funeral, while my family gathered in the living room of my grandmother's house and some of the men stood on the front porch and talked of violence, I walked through the woods on my grandmother's land. It was stifling inside the house, and loud with the sounds that accompany death, but outside it was cold and still. The air hovered right at freezing, and the light mist that fell could not decide whether it wanted to be snow or rain. Late in the afternoon, the dark came early, and by the time I turned around to walk back only the porch light was visible. The rain had finally made a decision, and the only sound around me was ice on frozen leaves.

I have never been in the house where it happened. The house is turned sideways to the road. The front yard is thick with trees and shrubs, blocking a clear view, but what you can see is a small rock house huddled on a quiet street in what might be any town. The front yard needs mowing, and the gutters are filled with leaves.

The inside of the house I must imagine, though in the years since the murder I have done the imagining enough times that the memories feel real. I start from the street, seeing the carport as it would have been that day—the stepfather's brown Chevy truck idling in the drive, smoke leaking from the exhaust. Just off the carport is the woodpile, and past the carport is a chain-link fence separating the house from the one next door, only a few feet away.

From the carport a door opens into the kitchen. The kitchen is narrow, with a green linoleum floor. Above the sink a window looks out on the backyard. Past the kitchen, moving farther into the house, is a small dining table, and past the dining table is the living room. A short hall opens off the living room, and two bedrooms are tucked into the back. The phone hangs on the wall beside the sliding glass door, in the transitional space between the kitchen/dining room and living room.

Because I have so few memories of my nephew, I sometimes create false ones. I replace Keith with images stolen from my own life, put him in the place of my older daughter rubbing spaghetti into her hair or riding her tricycle in the driveway. I picture his walker rattling across the hardwood floor of my grandmother's house as we sat at the table or watched TV, the same noise my older daughter made rattling across the linoleum of our kitchen. I see myself walking outside holding him sometime in the late fall, geese veering south overhead and the wind cold around us, Keith pointing at the geese much as my younger daughter pointed years later, eyes wide with wonder. I see my sister holding him, rocking back and forth to coax him to sleep, the same as I did with my daughters night after night for years. And I see Keith falling and bumping his head on the coffee table once. It was a minor accident, the kind my daughters had many times, but when my stepsister picked him up, she cried longer than he did, though I had no idea why she was crying until many years later.

If I can do it, if I can remember my nephew smiling or laughing or holding out his arms to be picked up, I can forget the cold morning, the truck idling outside and something happening that caused the stepfather to open and close his hands as he moved toward Keith. Instead I can imagine my nephew standing at the sliding glass door in diapers, watching the dogs play in the backyard, or huddling scared from fireworks on the Fourth; I can imagine him with his mother in a plastic wading pool she bought at Walmart, one with ducks on it, her son splashing her as she sits on the edge of the pool laughing; as a young boy running through the sprinkler in the backyard.

The last time I drove past, the house was empty. As far as I can remember it had always been rented, changing hands from one family to the next with the same regularity as the seasons. This was only a few years ago, and though I know the house hadn't been empty long and would not remain that way, in my mind it stands empty now. There is no dining table, no phone hanging from the wall. There is no sprinkler in the backyard, and no one to run through it.

My first daughter was born in the hospital where my nephew died. We lived in a small house at the time, on a small side street in a small town. When we brought my daughter home, my wife held her for days. At night we lay in bed together, the three of us, my daughter between us, her chest rising and falling rapidly, her lungs small and frail, and neither of us could sleep for fear of rolling over on her. Late at night I carried her to her crib, and my wife and I stood staring down at her. Later, when the house was quiet and everyone was asleep, I went out and stood in the backyard. It had snowed a few days earlier, and at some point I realized it was the anniversary of Keith's death, but I don't remember what I did there, or what I thought about, only that the stars were bright and the night was cold.

I have never told my wife this story. Lying in bed late at night I open my mouth to speak, then close it again. On the second floor above us, our daughters sleep. I wonder what they dream, if, when they get older, they will know the kind of fear that sometimes creeps into my heart.

When my first daughter was eighteen months old my wife came home from a routine doctor's visit crying. Our daughter's head was forming incorrectly, the doctors told her, the sutures misaligned. Her brain could be squeezed together, trapped between the bones of her skull. A few days later we took her for a CAT scan. My wife dug her fingernails into my arm as nurses slid our daughter, unconscious, into the machine. She was asleep for hours afterward. We sat in a little alcove, separated from the main room by a curtain. We could see the feet of nurses passing outside, and every few minutes one would stick her head through the curtain and check on us.

I don't remember the details of that little room, nor what my daughter was wearing. I remember her waking, and smiling, and the nurse coming to tell us that the CAT scan showed nothing abnormal. Afterward, we drove home, though I have forgotten what time of year it was, or how bright the snow might have been or if the sun were shining or if it were night, and sometimes I wonder that if there had been something wrong, how it would feel twenty years later. Would I have to dredge up the memories or would they come to me at times unbidden, moving from one to the next: her riding her tricycle in the driveway; shying away from the neighbor's dogs that barked at her; running through the sprinkler in the backyard.

There was no picture of the stepfather in the paper, just as there was no picture of Keith. What I have, I have had to recreate from memory. I hold hard to my re-creation of the little house because it is easier than understanding or forgiveness: the truck idling in the driveway, the stepfather's hands opening and closing, the ice on the roads as I drove to the hospital.

But sometimes a different memory creeps in, no matter what I do to keep it out. It is Thanksgiving, four months before Keith's death. We have gathered at my grandmother's house. We have eaten until we are sick, and now we lay back and watch football on TV, or else walk slowly in the yard to work off what we have eaten. It is damp, and cool. It has rained the night before.

I am standing in the kitchen, looking out onto the backyard through the sliding glass door. The stepfather is playing with Keith. The stepfather holds his hands up and growls like a monster. Keith laughs and tries to get away but he totters and falls. He is fourteen months old and has just learned to walk and the world beneath him is still shaky and suspicious. But when he falls the stepfather scoops him up and holds Keith above his head and Keith squeals with delight as the stepfather laughs. The boy's eyes are bright. When he laughs, I can see his front two teeth, just coming in.

I wish I were more forgiving. I wish the world made more sense sometimes. I wish some memories did not drive wedges through others, that a moment could be defined in sharper terms—black or white, love or hate, good or bad. I watch the game of chase, laughing with them, until the stepfather turns and sees me. He offers a little wave, and I wave back.

My stepfather has not spoken Keith's name in twenty years. But sometimes, in the years after it happened, before I moved away and went to college and then started a family of my own, I'd come home late at night and find him smoking in the dark of the living room. He never spoke to me on these nights, just nodded his head as I passed, the smell of his cigarette following me to my bedroom, where I would try to sleep. In bed, I'd think of him in there, smoke curling above him, headlights from the road occasionally sweeping the wall. I knew he was thinking of something. Some nights I'd climb out of bed and join him. We'd sit until very late, until morning was coming outside, both of us staring into whatever thoughts occupied us, whatever dreams we could not handle while asleep. We'd both be very quiet, listening to the silence gathering around us.

My family does not mention Keith. I wonder who visits his grave. I do not even know where it is. There was no graveside service, not until weeks later when the state medical examiner had outlined the history of violence on his body. I could find out, could make the long drive back to Arkansas and stand some November with the wind in the trees and the clouds racing above me and look down at his name. But I wonder if I would only be doing it for me—that whatever comfort provided by the act would be for me alone, and it saddens me to know this about myself.

Six months after we moved to North Carolina I rose past midnight and dressed. It had been snowing all day, and earlier my wife and I had taken our daughters out to make snow angels and snowmen and chase each other with snowballs. Late that night it was still snowing, the roads blanked out, everything bright in the reflected light. I walked to the university where I took graduate classes. My younger daughter was about the age Keith had been when he died. My older daughter was years older than he had ever been. On a small hill overlooking the soccer field, I knelt and watched the snow fall. There were no cars on the roads, no sounds passing in the night. The lights in the dorms and buildings were out, and it was easy to think I was alone in all the world. In the classes I teach, I have heard myself saying that winter often represents death, the world shriveling and dying, until spring comes and life bursts forth once again. When I get home I will lean over each of my daughters, my younger still in her crib, and when my wife wakes and finds me there, I will not be able to explain any of it to her.

The stepfather was sent to prison in December. I do not how it was arranged, if he was forced to turn himself in, if family members stood and watched him go, watched the handcuffs put on, watched him loaded in the back of the waiting car. He might have been forced to surrender himself the night before, and spend his last night in jail, but I know none of this. My imagining of how this occurred comes from prison movies, where white vans wired with steel mesh roll through gates topped with concertina wire, and the veteran prisoners whistle at the newcomers, who look around wild-eyed and frightened, while a burly guard with a shaved head slaps a nightstick into his palm.

Nor can I imagine the inside of the prison without a movie or TV show creeping in: a stacked tier where burning paper rains down on the normally stoic guards, or a yard where every space belongs to one gang or another, and even standing in the wrong place can lead to a violent attack, and though I was raised by forgiving people there are times when I feel he deserves a violent place, that there should be no forgiveness.

But at other times I can begin to find sympathy for him, if not exactly forgiveness. I see him sitting on the edge of the bed, elbows propped on his knees, staring at the wall. Or shuffling through the prison yard alone on a cold day in early February, or waking up in the middle of the night to a muffled sob, what might be a strange sound in a world of violent men, and wondering if he had made it.

I was the first to hold my older daughter, before the doctor, before my wife. We were on the fifth or sixth floor of the hospital, and I could see the city stretched out below, dingy in winter but ringed with blue hills all around. Her eyes were not open and she was crying like only a newborn can, but I held her near the window as if to show her the world she had come into.

The first year of her life is chronicled in pictures, and in each one I am holding her, or my wife is, or my mother or my brother, each of us with a hand cupped gently under her head. She grows larger in each one, until she is standing, holding onto the edge of a chair or the coffee table, then walking unsteadily from parent to parent. There are pictures of her fine blonde curls, of her riding a tricycle in the driveway, of her standing by a Japanese maple I planted in our front yard.

While she is growing, my mother comes to our house every day to see her. My stepfather makes strange faces at her and babbles like an idiot, something I have never seen him do. When I make fun of him for it, he tells me to shut up, then hugs me with enough strength to stretch my ribs and kisses me on the forehead, as if I am two years old. When we move to North Carolina, my parents fly in three or four times a year. By this time my wife and I have a second daughter, and our older starts kindergarten. We stand outside one hot August morning and watch her get on the bus. As the bus pulls away, my wife cries for several minutes, holding our younger and kissing her repeatedly.

When they are gone sometimes, when the morning is quiet, when my parents have not flown in unexpectedly, when I am turning some old memory over and over, trying to make sense of it, I dig through an old shoebox of photos. I go through the pictures one by one, seeing the linear and vertical progression of my daughters' lives, or myself, looking slightly older in each one, yet somehow less wise as the years go past.

In the pictures in my mind I see a house, a carport, a man coming home from work. His stepson is crying. The man is tired. He wants a drink and to sit in front of the TV, but the child is crying. The rattle doesn't work. The cartoons the child watches doesn't work either. The teething ring, the blue one with fishes on it, also does not work, so he reaches for the child, and what were cries before become something else entirely. Outside, the crunch of ice under tires.

Once, before my nephew's death, his stepfather brought him into the grocery store where I worked near closing time one night. Keith was crying, throwing his head back and screaming, and the stepfather had little idea what to do. I was a teenage boy then, and many years later, I would grow up to be a writer who spent a lot of time trying to make sense of the past. The stepfather looked frustrated or angry or even lost, so I held out my arms and Keith came to me and stopped crying. There were few people in the store so I wandered around talking to him while his stepfather bought cigarettes. He smelled fresh and clean and I thought we had something in common, though at the time I couldn't put a name to it, couldn't see that what we had in common was the life that lay ahead of us, both of them just beginning. In a few years I would be a young father holding a daughter for the first time, worried and scared for all the things in the world that could happen to her, but of course I knew none of that then. Winter had just set in and the dark came early and no one knew he had only a few months to live, and when I handed him back to his stepfather he started crying again, though it would have been impossible, I am sure, to have known the reason why.

MY POSSUM PROBLEM, AND HOW IT FINALLY ENDED

The first time I saw the possum I screamed and ran back inside. I had just stepped out for a midnight smoke, and when I opened the back door, the possum was heading for the hole under the back porch steps and under the house, where, I would later learn, it lived. We both paused mid-step. Its little possum eyes stared at me. Then I screamed and it squealed. I shot back inside the house and slammed the door and the possum shot under the stairs and into the hollow space beneath our house.

"What was that?" my wife said from the other room.

"Possum," I calmly informed her.

"Possum?" she said. I could hear her turning pages in her book. I knew it would be one of those books with a bare-chested man on the front, looming over a half-dressed woman. Either that or an alliterative detective novel whose author has either three names or two initials. It would not be a book about possums, which I decided I needed, as my mind had begun to consider rabies, and my two daughters sleeping upstairs.

"Possum," I confirmed.

"Was it cute?" she said.

I rolled my eyes, then realized she couldn't see me. "*Cute* is not a word I would have thought of first," I told her.

I spent the next few hours, until dawn or so, peering out the window, or smoking with the door slightly open. Before my wife went to bed she yelled from the bedroom, asking if I was smoking in the house. She doesn't like me smoking, and I am strictly forbidden from doing so in the house, but this was different.

"There's a possum out there," I said.

"Give it a cigarette," she said. Her light went out. Our two daughters were already asleep upstairs, so I decided to sleep on the couch near the back door, in case the possum tried to crawl under the door or force it open, although I didn't actually sleep until my wife and children were awake the next morning, after dawn had convinced me the possum wasn't going to sneak in the back door and kill us in our sleep.

A few days later I saw the possum again. I had forgotten about it, and wandered outside. It was sitting a few feet away. It began hissing at me. I didn't quite scream, but I did run inside, slamming the door after me.

"What are you doing?" my wife said, and "Possum," I replied.

"Again?"

"It's looking for something," I told her, then realized it was true. I watched it wander around the backyard. There's something unnerving about a possum—the hairless tail, the beady eyes. After a while it went under the house. All night, I thought I could hear it.

When we were kids, my brother had a gerbil that constantly got out of its cage. I suspect now my brother was letting it out on purpose. He didn't like keeping it caged, but was afraid to let it go for fear it would get outside and one of our dogs would eat it. This might seem a strange fear, but we had once seen a dog eat a mouse. Our father raised hunting dogs, and in our old barn we found a tiny little mouse shivering in a corner of one of the empty stalls. My father sicced the dog on it, and the dog snapped and swallowed the mouse. It was so small it must have been a baby, and when my brother and I began to cry, our father told us that mice were filthy creatures that carried all kinds of diseases, but my brother and I hated him a little and for a long time afterward the image of the mouse huddled in fright, then gone, stuck sharp in our minds.

When the gerbil got loose, we'd be watching TV in the living room and see it streak across the floor. My mother would scream and climb up on the couch, then yell at my brother to catch it. We would spend the next few hours chasing it around the house, until finally one of us dropped a shoebox on top of it and scooped it back into the cage.

Sometimes, when it got out, the gerbil crawled into the walls of the house. We could hear it running and chewing and scratching. We would come home from school to find little piles of sawdust below holes in the baseboards where it had made a new home. One night, half-asleep, it jumped on me, and I woke screaming. Not long after that my stepfather put out mousetraps, and we never saw the gerbil again.

I was thinking of the gerbil while I tried to sleep, afraid I would wake with a possum sitting on my chest. Or that possums could climb through the walls like the gerbil did, and somehow reach the second floor, where it would stalk across the floor toward my sleeping daughters, its eyes red in the nightlight. To prevent such a thing from happening, I locked the back door, then went to bed. But sometimes our minds become irrational when thinking about protecting our children, and locking the door didn't satisfy me. I knew there was no way to fill in the space between the walls with concrete, at least not this late at night, but after a little while I did get up and throw the deadbolt.

I was sure I could hear it crawling beneath the house. Before going outside I began to look for it, and once when it was crawling around the backyard, but far enough away as to constitute no threat, I called my daughters downstairs and we eased the back door open to watch.

The first time she saw the possum, my younger daughter asked if it was a badger.

"No," I said. "Remember, just now, when I said 'Hey, come look at the possum'?"

They were standing bent over, the older looking over the younger's shoulder, both of them peering at the possum ten feet away.

"How do you know it's not a badger?" My younger daughter was ten or eleven at the time, and wanted everything to be magical, or at least out of the ordinary. I had thought a possum in the backyard would be not-ordinary enough, but apparently I was wrong. As I often am.

"Because it's not," I said.

"But how do you know?"

"Because a badger would have charged us and eaten us by now."

They both looked at me, attempting to ascertain if I were lying or not, finally deciding I was. But they scooted back inside a bit. We watched as it crept around.

"It's so cute," my younger daughter said.

"It could be rabid," I told her. "Or hungry. Starving enough to eat a human. Don't ever touch it, or get near it, or look at it."

"We're looking at it now," she pointed out.

"You know what I mean," I told her.

"Almost never," she said, and I contemplated throwing her to the hungry, rabid possum.

A few nights later I went outside and the possum was lying on a tree branch that hung near the back door. Its eyes turned red in the porch light.

I looked around for a stick but couldn't find one. The possum lay on the branch, watching me. Possums have a neat trick when confronted with danger, and that is to play dead, lying completely still, usually curled up on their backs with their feet in the air.

This possum was not playing dead. I didn't know whether to find something to attack it with or try to scare it away by flapping my arms and saying "go away," so finally I just sat down on the back porch steps and lit a cigarette. Upstairs, my daughters' light went out. I blew smoke at the possum. It didn't move.

I finished my cigarette and went back inside, but I couldn't focus on the movie I had been watching, as I was now thinking of the possum lying on the branch. I didn't know if possums could jump or climb like squirrels, but I imagined it leaping from the branch to the roof of our house, where it could walk to the window of my daughters' second-story room and peer in at them sleeping with the covers over their heads to protect them from monsters.

We live in the middle of the city, but often see wild animals. Raccoons slink around to forage through trash cans. Black widows nest in my smoker, my grill, and near the dryer vent outside the house. I've seen deer crossing the busy street near my house, and cranes drinking from the stream.

I've never lived in a house with a possum. In some places, people catch them and eat them, barbecued, or grilled. The tail, in some cultures, is a delicacy. When I suggested we capture and eat the possum, my wife patted me on the chest.

"Go right ahead," she said.

Later, in bed, I saw her looking at me out of the corner of her eye, wondering, perhaps, if she had married the kind of person who would execute and then devour a possum, with or without sauce.

My friend Julie, who lives a few blocks away, told me she was grading papers one night with the door propped open so her cat could go in and out. When she looked up, a baby possum was crawling across her floor. She took a picture and posted it on Facebook. I told her about my possum. We speculated as to whether or not there was an ongoing possum invasion of our neighborhood.

Last year, squirrels almost killed our cable guy. My internet wasn't working, and I could not look at YouTube videos or research tuberculosis or see pictures of possums posted on Facebook or any of the other things I do to keep from working, to keep from venturing out into the real world, where real problems exist and terrible things sometimes happen, so I called the cable company.

The next day one of their service men showed up. I explained the problem. He went out back to check the cable box, and when he started unscrewing the bolt holding it closed, power surged through the box. From inside the house, we heard popping noises.

The cable guy cursed and jumped back from the box, shaking his hand. He hadn't been touching the bolt, but the nearness of his hand had shocked him anyway. He said, "That damn near killed me."

He peered at the cable box from a distance. The electric meter on the house had stopped spinning, and all the power to the house was off. The singed smell of electrical wires drifted out from the house.

"Call the power company," he said, still rubbing his hand. He left shaking his head.

Inside the house, the smell of electrical smoke hung thick. A gray haze drifted through the house.

When the power guys got there and looked things over they told me squirrels had chewed through the electrical wires that grounded the house, and the power had been grounded through the cable box. When the cable guy had tried to unscrew the bolt, the power tried to surge through him.

They spent a few hours on a cold Sunday afternoon running new lines to the house, trimming tree limbs, and cursing squirrels.

"Squirrels will chew through anything," the older of the two told me. He wore a brown coverall and a green hat. His hair was white beneath the hat, and his hands were large and red, with big knuckles. "Fucking tree rats," he said, as if a squirrel had once injured a family member or bitten a small child in his neighborhood.

"Are you sure it wasn't a possum?" I said.

They looked at me as if I were daft.

"Possums don't do anything," the younger one said, looking at me from atop a ladder leaned against the side of the house, his hands full of wires. "Maybe shit under your house." He went back to stringing wire. "It was a squirrel."

"It's always a squirrel," the older one said. He cracked his knuckles. I thought of arthritis. "I've seen them chew through live wires. They eat the protective covering on the wires, then, sometimes, chew the wire itself to file their teeth."

"How do I keep them from doing it again?" I asked.

The older one looked around, as if to see if anyone else was listening.

"I'd kill every last one of them," he said. "Shoot the fuckers in the head, if I were you."

I did not consider shooting the possum. After initially scaring me, it hadn't done anything other than wander around the backyard on certain nights, pulling itself slowly through the grass, running away if I scared it. I was still not used to having a wild animal living in the crawl spaces beneath the house, but as long as it didn't come up the basement stairs and somehow open the door, I thought I could live with it.

I considered naming it, but did not know what an appropriate name for a possum would be: Cornelius? Napoleon? Nitroglycerin?

My daughters never named our cat. When we first got her they kicked names around for a few days, throwing out Princess and Fluffy and Beauregard, shooting down my offers of

Attila and Cheesefries and Agamemnon. We finally settled on Kitty, which was what we had been calling her since we got her, and which satisfied me because I like the movie *Big Jake* where John Wayne has a dog named "Dog."

One night I woke to find Kitty clawing and scratching at the door, her back up, making that weird growl-whine noise cats make when they are mad or scared or both. I turned on the porch light and looked out to see the possum sitting on the porch steps. Kitty had turned feral, spitting and scratching, her eyes as wild as I have ever seen them, and I wondered then how cats are any different from possums or squirrels or raccoons, other than the thousands of years of domestication, which then led me to wonder about our fear of small furry things that don't belong to the cat family. Why will we feed a stray cat but not a stray possum? And why, when I see a stray cat in the neighborhood, I do not think first of rabies, as I do with possums, and raccoons, and squirrels, although, as I have pointed out, squirrels do not necessarily need rabies to kill the cable guy.

My younger daughter saw me peering out the window one night and came and joined me. I put my arm around her as we watched the possum sniff around the backyard.

After a few minutes she said, "Can we catch it?"

"No. It might have rabies. Even if it doesn't, it might bite."

She watched for a few more minutes. "It looks lonely."

I could feel the thin bones of her shoulders beneath my arm, her heart beating in her frail chest. "It's not lonely. It's a possum."

She looked at me, her eyes the same color as mine. "Possums don't get lonely?"

A strand of hair had fallen from where she hooked it behind her ears. "They're animals."

"So are we," she said, and I was forced to agree, but kept my thoughts to myself. I would argue that since we wear pants we get to be more important than lower creatures, but that may be my animal-prejudice rearing up. Also, does wearing pants mean we do not get lonely? Or that creatures without them don't as well?

In the six years we've lived in this house, our backyard has grown smaller. When we first moved, it was the size of a gas station or a dance floor. There's a small hill behind the house, and bamboo grows on the side of the hill. I like the Asian feeling, so over the years I've let the bamboo slowly and steadily march down the hill. I am also lazy when it comes to yard work, and each time I mow the backyard, I mow a little bit less, allowing the bamboo shoots and kudzu to creep a little farther in, so now the backyard is about the size of a college dorm room. The kudzu adds a Southern feel, which mixes with the bamboo so that the backyard seems both Asian and Southern. I am thinking of adding a koi pond but stocking it with catfish, or crappie.

There's a thin strip of trees that runs behind our house, and all down the block. It's not much, but a tiny divider between houses, so that in the spring and summer, when the leaves are full on the trees, we can't see the houses behind us. I grew up in rural Arkansas, and the trees in the backyard screening me from other houses are welcome.

I suppose they are welcome to the possum too. I know wild animals adapt easily to life in the city, but began to wonder if cutting down all the trees and bush-hogging the backyard would make the possum feel unwanted.

My wife spends much less time thinking about the possum than I do. My daughters are the same way. After the first time I showed the possum to them, they became uninterested. I would see it in the backyard and rush to tell them.

"Is it the possum again?" my older said.

"No," I told her. "It's a giant rabbit wreaking havoc around the neighborhood, eating small children."

She rolled her eyes and went back to doing homework.

"We've seen it," my younger daughter said, equally non-excited. She was curled on the couch reading, and she is hard to talk to when she is reading, reluctant to pull herself out of the world she has entered.

"But it's cute," I reminded her. "Remember?"

She didn't look up. "You said it had rabies."

"Might," I said. "Might have rabies. But it doesn't."

She read for a moment, then marked her spot with a finger. "How do you know?"

"If it had rabies, it would have eaten you," I said.

She put her face back in her book. "It would have eaten you first," she said, to which I could not argue.

I came home from the bar late one night and went out back to smoke. I was sitting in my smoking chair when I saw the possum's head peek out from under the stairs. It crept halfway out of the hole, and sat there. I'd had seven or eight too many drinks, but I swear it was looking at me, waiting for something. After a while it backed into the hole beneath the stairs and disappeared. I saw its tail as it turned around, and then it was gone.

"What do you want?" I said, but it didn't answer. I'm not sure if it was because it didn't want to talk about it, or if it didn't want to talk to someone who might not remember the conversation in the morning.

A few months after I first saw the possum I went down into the basement to empty the drainage bucket. Our basement is unfinished. The hot water heater stands in the middle of the room. The basement walls are cinderblock, usually sweating, and you can see into the crawl spaces under the house. Spiderwebs hang everywhere, and huge cicadas with armored carapaces and bulbous eyes and knees that bend the wrong way cling to the sweating walls.

We don't go down there often. But water seeps in sometimes after a hard rain. Our landlords have been trying to fix the problem, and so started a plumbing system made of PVC pipe to channel the water into a drain in the concrete floor, but when I went down it had not been finished yet, and there was only a short length of pipe coming through a hole in the wall. When it rained, water came through the pipe and into a collecting bucket, which I had to empty after every rain.

The basement smelled of must and damp, as it always does, but the smell seemed thicker, heavier. I stood in the middle of the small room and looked up under the house for where the possum hid at night, then wondered what I would do if I actually found it, and decided that getting out of the basement would be the best course of action.

When I went to pick up the bucket I saw the little possums floating in it. They must have crawled through the pipe when the weather turned cold two weeks ago, and fallen into the bucket. I stood there trying to remember when it last rained, trying to calculate when I first saw the mother possum wandering around in the backyard as if she were looking for something.

Their bodies had bloated in the water. The surface was slick with oil secreted from their carcasses. Their eyes were open. They were tiny things, each smaller than a mouse, floating in the foul-smelling water.

I imagined the mother possum, circling the house night after night, wondering where her children had gone. I think maybe she was looking for help, someone to get them out, because she could not, but I don't know if possums think that way. Did she watch the water rising, her brood trying to stay afloat? I don't know. Somewhere above me, my children were climbing into bed, or just waking up, or brushing their teeth or getting dressed or watching TV or a thousand other things they do up there, unaware of all the dangers their parents see lurking in the world.

I didn't tell my wife about the possum, or the babies bloated and drowned in the bucket. I didn't want her to think of them down there, or of the mother circling our backyard night after night, looking for them. Knowing about it would make her sad, so I didn't say anything. I didn't want her to be the one who went upstairs a dozen times every night to check on our daughters and make sure nothing had come up the stairs after them or they hadn't somehow slipped into something we could not get them out of.

I do it, and let her sleep.

THE WILD THING
WITH PEOPLE FEET
WAS MY FAVORITE

I liked the way he hung from the trees, his big feet dangling. The other wild things had beaks and long claws, scaly or feathery or rubbery webbed chicken feet. One had a parrot-head, one had a beard, and one had long reddish hair. One had a big nose smashed flat and a fat belly like the old men at the cafe my father hid out in Sunday mornings when he was trying to avoid my mother. One was smaller than the others and looked like a goat, but I liked the people-footed wild thing best, his horns, his gray fur, his square white teeth. I liked the dark landscape lurking on each page, the wall of trees, the big sky and carved moon, the ocean Max sailed across, in and out of weeks, for almost over a year, which seemed a very long time when I was four.

I'm sure my mother read the story to me first, but I remember my year-older brother turning the pages, forming the words, forming the world out of the words. In the old worn copy I still have, he wrote out lessons to teach me to read and write, jumbled sentences, syntax thrown off, whether to use *lie* or *lay, rise* or *raise,* and when I finished each exercise he graded them with a purple marker, though neither of us understood, at four and five, that sentences could take more than one form, words could be arranged in more than one way.

When we weren't rearranging sentences we drew monsters on the blank pages before the story starts, before Max is sent to his room without any supper, before he made mischief of the worst kind by chasing his dog with a fork and driving nails into the wall. Our mother caught us once, and took the book away, and we sat cross-armed and frowning in our room. That night while she cooked in the kitchen I thought about Max yelling "I'll eat you up" like a curse before sailing off, the moon above him hung like wax, the little waves slapping at the boat. I always imagined that she would be sorry when she came to check on him and he was gone, that she would wail and gnash her teeth and cry.

The monsters we drew were attempts to recreate the beaks and horns and people-feet of the wild things, the suggestion of danger in their big wide eyes. They seemed, the ones Mr. Sendak drew, to have some secret knowledge of the dim places of the world, as if a child's imagination runs to darkness. Sometimes, late at night, the TV flickering blue from the other room, throwing my parents' shadows on the walls as their nightly argument grew, I thought of the land of the wild things as full of dark promises, a place where we could be what we held in our secret hearts, could let loose the anger we sometimes felt—at our mother, our father, our brother who tried to stifle the sentences we felt inside us, anyone who would not let us be what we wanted to be.

The one with people feet, I thought, had once been human, but had changed. He grew wild. Everyone grew wild at times, from the Baptist preacher down the road who told us we were going to Hell when he worked up to the pinnacle of his sermon, to my brother who threatened to run away over the hill behind our house when he grew angry, to my mother and father when their words turned sharp and they aimed them at one another like claws. He had grown wild, his once-human body sprouting horns and gray fur, eyes yellowing, only his people-feet left now. Like the others, he roared and gnashed and bit and stomped and swung from the trees and howled at the moon.

Or perhaps he was monster becoming more human. We did not know if Max were becoming more like a monster or teaching the wild things to be more like him. It seemed important. Out the windows of our room a peach tree that bore no fruit was wrapped in webs that would eventually kill it, tiny caterpillars writhing beneath the thin silk. Frost hung in the fields as our father left and our mother smoked one cigarette after another in the living room. Sumac shone red in the cold morning. Behind the house the woods closed in, a place that seemed as dark as the forest that grew in Max's room, and, when I got older, I would walk through to hear the silence of my own heart, much as Max imagines a world waiting for him, a place where there are no rules or regulations, and all the inhabitants are as hard and wild as he wishes to be.

The wild things have claws and teeth, but Max, not much older than those who first come in contact with the book, tames them all with the magic trick of staring into their eyes without blinking once, and there is for me in these lines the idea that humans have the greatest capacity for wildness. They call Max the wildest of the wild things, and name him king and carry him on their shoulders, and when he tells them he is leaving they threaten to eat him out of love. I didn't know when I first read the book about love that could consume you, not until my daughters came crying into the world, but there was in the words a darkness that seemed to linger in the shadows of the trees, and I guessed even then that love could be so strong as to lead to hate, worry to anger, that evil is often more alluring, the suggestion of what would happen to Max if he let the wildness take over.

He leads them in the wild rumpus, and afterward sends them off to bed without any supper, handing out the same treatment he received, for the same reason, imposing the same rules he sought to escape. He has grown lonely. Not even the people-feeted wild thing can help him, for it is only a wild thing, a thing conjured out of the dark places of our hearts, when we grow wild and angry and make mischief of one kind and another.

Eventually, smelling the food from faraway lands, Max decides to leave. He wants to be where someone loves him best of all, and though the wild things roar and gnash and stomp and howl, Max climbs into his boat and sails back over a year, in and out of weeks and through a day and into the night of his very own room, where he finds forgiveness from his mother in the form of his supper waiting for him.

The entire text is 339 words. Barely a single typed page. The people-footed monster is shown seven times, and in each one he wears a different expression, from sleeping to gnashing to jumping at the moon, all the poles of human emotions, the wild swing from sadness to joy to despair. When my daughters were younger I pointed out the wild thing's people feet dozens of times, along with the little goat wild thing that is the same size and same color as Max. All of the monsters have some human characteristic, even the fat one and the duck-footed one and the one in the sea that breathes hot air on Max's boat, but I never asked my daughters if the wild things were human turning into monster, or monster becoming human. I find myself afraid of the answer now. The wild things are everywhere, with their big eyes and claws and horns. They roar their terrible roars and gnash their terrible teeth, although we only recognize our own voices, our own weapons, see ourselves in their big yellow eyes. It is easy to forget the story is imagination when we can see the wildness of ourselves everywhere, in cities where the dead lie in the streets while bombs go off in the distance, or in elementary schools where gunshots ring out and children scream in terror, and some nights I wonder which we are, which way we are turning, if we are coming out of the darkness or sailing straight for it.

On the front cover of the book there is only the sleeping people-footed wild thing, and Max's empty boat. On the back cover there is only the moon, the little stream rushing by, a few trees and a flower. As if everyone has gone, and only the empty night remains, the moon hung like a chalk mark. It is interesting to note that the title is neither a question nor a statement, but a wondering, something in-between, half one, half the other.

When my parent's marriage fell apart they became like wild things themselves as they stood in the kitchen banging on the counters, their eyes as hard as the sentences they hurled at one another. There is no father in the story, and after mine left I read the book again, trying to understand why. After the divorce we moved to a different house, one that seemed empty and lonely and full of despair, *Where the Wild Things Are* packed away with the other books we had outgrown and only occasionally got out to read, nights when the moon came over the blue hills like a sail, full enough to throw silver light down on the world. After we moved my brother and I wished for some escape from where we had ended up and I began to drink a lot when I felt hopelessness settle in on me, the belief that I would never find a place to soothe the wild anger that often flared up inside me. When my children were born I sometimes heard my voice grow hard, and I wondered what I looked like to them, if I were turning into a monster, eyes wild, hands curled into claws.

The book sits in the attic now, its bindings broken, all the pages colored on. Max's eyes have been stabbed out in some of the pictures, but the monsters still stare at us with their big yellow orbs as if they have something to tell us. I am still trying to rearrange sentences into some sort of order, still trying to find the right verbs, the right syntax to convey meaning in and out of weeks and through the years. Mr. Sendak is gone, and late some nights my heart grows dark and I wish for a wax moon to rise out the window, for trees to grow in my room. My children are no longer small enough to hold. They no longer sit in my lap and listen to my growling voice as I read the wilds things' words, they no longer point out the wild thing with people feet. They read by themselves now, and sometimes the monsters and darknesses of the world call to them and they grow angry or sad or depressed. But they still sleep above us, and most nights I am not filled with my own hurt and worry, so I climb the stairs to their room and smooth the hair back from their warm foreheads. Then I go through the house turning off all the lights, and stand there in the darkness listening, wondering why anyone would ever wish to leave such a place.

THE NIGHT
BEFORE CHRISTMAS

My parents live at the edge of a small Arkansas town. Their house sits atop a hill, and across the low valley other hills spread out like bruises. The valley has turned brown now with winter, and under the gray days the land lays dormant, the gray wind whistling over mountain flanks.

This is the town I grew up in, the town where both my daughters were born. Eleven years ago I left Arkansas for North Carolina, and the town has slowly changed in my absence. Many of the businesses down main street are boarded over. Restaurants stay open for only a few months before the new owners decide to close, and, a few months later, when new owners buy the place, they will only stay open a few months as well. The recession has hit hard here. The town's biggest factories have closed—one because of fire, and one because of sluggish, or no, economic growth—and jobs are scarce. The car dealerships are gone, or failing. The movie theater has been closed for three years for renovations, and many people here suspect it will never re-open.

Past my parents' house the road turns to dirt as the town ends. There are no other houses around. The woods close

33

in, thick brush and heavy trees leaning over the road. Grass grows in the middle of the road where tires have not worn a path. At night, the road turns dark away from the streetlights and house lights and TVs spilling blue light onto the front yards of the quiet houses.

At the bottom of the hill the road ends. Pastureland begins, a small creek running through, brown cattle worrying the winter grass. From the top of the hill you can follow the winding curve of the creek. Across the pasture, more hills rise up, ringing us in.

At night, cars creep up and down the road, lights blacked out. If you listen, as I do when I am here visiting, sitting on the porch in the cold winter wind or the not-quite-cool nights of summer, you can hear hurried conversations, the quiet opening and closing of doors, hands held over interior car lights to shut them out. Lights, visibility, are not welcome here. People dump stray dogs along the road all the time, and they wander over to my parents' neighbors' house. The neighbors are kind and gentle-hearted people, and they take in a half-dozen strays a year. People dump trash on the road, and old furniture, and once, last summer, when my stepfather was walking down the dirt road with my older daughter, he found an old 12-volt flashlight someone had thrown out. He thought he would fix it, so he climbed into the weeds at road's edge and took it home. When he opened the casing he found four plastic bags of crystal meth.

We came this year close to Christmas, driving west from North Carolina, across the Appalachians and the long stretch of Tennessee where strip malls hold the same stores and restaurants in every city, every little town. Our first afternoon here my father and I drove for hours through the countryside, along dirt roads where the brown pastures spread to either side, small strands of trees stripped of leaves. The winter sun reflected off the metal roofs of chicken houses, the surface of small orange ponds where cattle leaned over to drink, their breath fanning the air before them. My father pointed out places he had hunted as a child, old houses worn down to the foundation, trees growing through the ruins, houses worn by time and wind. He did not mention the other houses we saw, the burned-out remnants of trailer houses and old clapboard houses set back from the road, the charred signature of smoke where fire curled from the blackened windows.

In town, we drove past the old ice plant, where men sawed blocks of ice in the days before refrigeration. He asked me if I remembered it. I only remember the old brick building, already abandoned by the time I was born, vines crawling over the structure, doors and windows gone, and as we continue to drive past abandoned buildings and boarded-over storefronts, I wonder if he is remembering the town as it used to be. Even in the decade I have been gone the town has changed dramatically. When the factories failed the jobs ended, and on some small streets there are more houses empty than occupied. Hand-lettered "For Sale" signs hang in dirty windows. Old cars in the yards gather weeds.

But driving past the city limits the population sign tells me more people live here than ever. They have moved to new subdivisions on the edge of town, away from the center, much as happens in some inner cities. I think of all the pictures and stories I've seen from Detroit in the last few years, the ruin-porn, the endless coverage of a dying city. The fires. The emptying of the inner city. The rampant drugs. I am far from the Rust Belt of America, but the same circumstances have been recreated here: factories closing down, people fleeing for better opportunities. And those who stay are forced to try to make a living where there is no living to be had.

The town has always struggled to find work. It was founded in 1828, when a man named Walter Cauthron opened a general store near the Petit Jean River. In the 1800s the only industry to be found was farming, a general store, a cotton gin, a blacksmith for shoeing horses. Most of the land in the area was devoted to raising cattle or crops. The town itself consisted of a main street with a few storefronts, until the railroad came through in 1898 and the population began to rise with the new-found industry. The railroad bought the surrounding land and sold it in farming sections. More people came. Not long after the railroad arrived, the Arkansas State Tuberculosis Sanatorium was built on Potts Hill just south of town. The new jobs brought more people. As did the tuberculosis. Many of those released from the sanatorium stayed in the town, either to start a new life or to work at the sanatorium and help others suffering from the disease.

During the Depression and World War II, the town struggled again. Crops failed under the clouds of dust that blew east from Oklahoma. Men were drafted for service and women moved away to work in the factories. They stayed gone until the '50s, when the town formed the Industrial Development Committee to attract industry and bring jobs to the area. In the '50s and '60s, new plants opened. Retirees returned, attracted to small-town Southern life. More factories moved in. The tuberculosis sanatorium closed, but re-opened as a home for the developmentally disabled.

I was born in the early '70s. I remember the country's bicentennial. Parades down main street. A state football championship in the mid-'80s, about the time Reagan threatened to close down the state-run institute where my mother and stepfather worked, and we contemplated moving to the suburbs of a larger city. Summer nights we circled town like the stars swimming through the big sky river, or stood on the rural bridge where kids dare each other to jump after a few beers. Someone got busted for pot, drinking too much, or driving after drinking too much. They were arrested for little things like breaking into the swimming pool on hot summer nights or throwing a beer bottle at a road sign. In health classes we watched videos about the dangers of drugs, Nancy Reagan had started the D.A.R.E. campaign, and we heard about crack in the inner cities, which seemed so far removed from us in our small Southern town we never worried about it.

We did not know that out West, methamphetamines had spread through the streets of Portland and Seattle and the cities in Northern California, heading east. It was first synthesized in 1919 in Japan. During World War II millions of tablets were handed out to forces on both sides to fight fatigue and hunger. In the 1950s Japanese industrial workers used it to increase productivity. In the '60s crystal meth became popular with truckers on long hauls, with bikers driving cross-country. (They carried it in their crank cases, from which the name "crank" derived.) In the '30s and '40s meth was sold in a number of popular over-the-counter drugs, and prescribed for various treatments ranging from narcolepsy to alcoholism to obesity. By the '70s it was a controlled substance. By the '90s people, lots of people, were making it in their homes. Instructions on how to manufacture meth proliferated on the Internet, and can still be found there. So can pictures of what happens to people who use it. In the late '80s police in Oregon began keeping records on meth use when they started seeing the same people return to jail again and again, slightly altered each time—fewer teeth, less hair, more scratches and lines on their faces. They began finding more and more home labs. By the time houses began to explode all over the Pacific Northwest, they were using the word *epidemic*.

As my father and I drive, there are fires everywhere. People burning trash or leaves in their yards, leaning on rakes, nodding as we pass by. The weather is warm for this time of year, hovering in the mid-50s. A good time to burn leaves, to stand outside under the winter-slanted sun, watch the hawks circling high on drafts of air, nod to cars as they come by. Driving along the country roads we see a hawk swoop down on a field mouse, carry it off in its talons. We see wild turkeys crossing the road, a roadrunner, hundreds of squirrels, a doe bending to drink at a small creek winding through pastureland. We see children fishing along a small creek in the almost-warm afternoon.

In other places, away from town or on certain streets, everything seems dead. The world has not ended on December 21st, but the town seems deserted, abandoned, and it is only a short step to imagining all the houses burned or emptied. That night, the temperature drops below freezing, and on the local news I hear that cold nights near Christmas carry the greatest chance of fire because of all the lights and electrical outlets overloaded, the paper strewn everywhere, the roaring fire.

The news says nothing of chemicals cooking.

Common ingredients in crystal meth include acetone, used in nail polish remover and paint thinner; lithium, which was used as a fusion fuel in early hydrogen bombs; and toluene, which can be used as an industrial solvent, inhalant, or octane booster in racing fuel. Also used are hydrochloric acid, sodium hydroxide, sulfuric acid, and anhydrous ammonia, along with red phosphorous, the stuff that ignites matches.

All of the ingredients are highly flammable and unstable. Taken alone, or in a cooking environment, they can cause respiratory problems, skin irritation, migraines, death. When police clean out a meth house, they wear respirators, Tyvek suits, eye goggles, shoe coverings, and gloves. (Many police officers who cleaned out labs in the '60s and '70s, before the dangers were known, now suffer health problems directly related to inhaling cooking fumes.) Since 1998, in Missouri, only a few hundred miles north of my hometown, police have seized 12,354 meth labs, 251,000 pounds of solid waste, and 118,000 pounds of toxic waste.

In 2011, the DEA registered over 10,000 meth lab incidents, where either chemicals or cookware were found. Besides the sometimes as high as 20% of meth labs that explode, thousands of houses are sold without the buyers being aware the house was formerly used for cooking meth. Few states have laws that require lab houses to be cleaned. There has been no national study on how clean is clean, and in those states that do have laws, cleaning a house where meth was cooked may be as simple as airing the house out for a few days and repainting the room used for cooking.

From 2004 to 2009, the DEA found 1,789 meth labs in hotels. I use the word *found,* because those are only the ones they found. That's out of three million rooms rented nightly. For five years. The hotel owners are often reluctant to report the labs because it will mean a costly cleanup. I will think of this statistic when we stop at a hotel in Tennessee, the state with the second-highest number of meth lab seizures. I will wonder if they have re-painted the room and aired it out.

Christmas morning, before the snow comes, before we gather in warm houses to eat and drink and laugh, my brother and I take another drive through the streets of town. We are seeing sights, as my father and I did a few days before, but the sights we are seeing are not for pleasure, this time. I have a list of addresses where police raided drug labs, and as we move slowly through the gray morning, my brother reading the addresses and me reading the street signs, I think of how close the scourge has come, how easily we can be reached. The church bells ring the morning and geese fly overhead and here we are, driving through a town we grew up in, have loved and hated and every shade of emotion in between, looking for drug houses among the houses we have driven past all our lives.

The first house is no longer there. The data I have lists a discovered lab at the address in 2004, but there is no house, only an empty lot, grown over with weeds. On another day I might have gotten out of the car and searched for clues, but I don't need clues—I know what has happened here.

Both the second and third houses on the list are less than a mile away from my mother's house. I could walk to either one of them in less than five minutes. As a child, I rode my bike past both of them a hundred times. They are both small, and run-down. A small shed out back, a dirt driveway, sheets over the cracked windows. There are toys—a bicycle, a football—in the front yard. Both were raided in 2007, and though there are no signs of meth cooking now—no chemical fumes, no clandestine cars streaking in and pulling rapidly away, no furtive glances out the windows of the house—my brother, who has worked in the medical field for most of his life and now counsels teenagers, thinks of health first, of people living in a house where meth was cooked, chemicals soaking into walls and floors and carpeting and curtains. He thinks of children playing in rooms where poison was made.

"My god," he says. "Those poor kids."

He is more right than he knows. Thirty percent of seized labs have had children living in them. In some states, over 50% of children in protective services come from meth lab seizures. Even now, the long-term effects of meth on children are unknown. My older daughter was with my stepfather when he found the flashlight with the meth hidden inside. When I walked down the road past the spot the day before Christmas, I could hear children calling to each other just a few houses away.

The fourth house on the list is gone, as is the fifth. They are both empty lots, the fourth a few houses down from my best friend's grandmother's house, a house we used to go to after school to watch cartoons we were too old to be watching. It is two blocks from the elementary school, the library, the school superintendent's office. The church bells ring again. Clouds pass overhead. We hear a police siren in the distance and look at each other, both thinking the same thing. The fifth house is across the street from a church. It's three houses away from the woman who babysat my older daughter before we moved to North Carolina. It is across the street from the baseball field where I played Little League, where bats veered through the park lights over the center field position where I stood on so many summer nights, listening to my parents and friends and friends' parents cheer from the old wooden bleachers.

The last address is two houses away from my grandmother's house, where she has lived for close to fifty years. Like several of the others, the house is no longer there. From the empty lot my brother and I can see the rest of our family gathering at my grandmother's house.

My mother came home from work one day to find the propane tank on her gas grill stolen. When she called the police, they told her it was stolen to cook meth. One policeman told her of rolling labs, where the backs of trucks are used, especially dangerous because of the jostling as the truck turns, as it bounces over shaky roads and the chemicals spill into one another. He told her cookers will set up in the middle of the woods and cook for a few days, then dump all the chemicals, where they seep into the groundwater, into creeks where people swim in summer.

"It's everywhere," he said.

I keep coming back to numbers. Over 10,000 drug lab incidents in 2011. Most of them in Missouri and Tennessee and Oklahoma and Arkansas. Almost 12,000 in 2010. 13,000 in 2005. The numbers dropped slightly—only 6,000 incidents reported in 2007—after the 2005 Combat Methamphetamine Epidemic Act, but the numbers have risen again.

And these are the small operations. Home cooking accounts for about 15% of total meth in the United States. The other 85% comes from super labs supplied and operated by Mexican drug cartels. They get ephedrine and pseudoephedrine—which the 2005 Combat Methamphetamine Epidemic Act made available only with a prescription—from rogue manufacturing plants in Eastern Europe and distribute it everywhere.

Near the center of town, on the wall of a closed-down car dealership now owned by the First Baptist Church, a twenty-foot high mural lists the Ten Commandments. Across the street, near the courthouse, the Methodist Church, which is the tallest building in town, is missing a stained-glass window, plywood covering the hole like an empty socket.

As we drive in late at night on the 21st, the town seems angelic. Christmas lights hang from poles along main street. There are few cars on the road. I have not been home for three years. I point out to my children familiar landmarks— the toy factory I worked in one summer before a round of layoffs, the bus depot where I left for Basic Training only a few months before Saddam Hussein invaded Kuwait and the first Gulf War began, the golf course where I worked for several years while failing at college.

We have been on the road all day and are bone-tired from the drive, but instead of turning toward my parents' house, I keep driving, past the hospital both my grandfathers died in, past the new addition at the edge of town and the old addition across the street from it where a high school friend had a basketball goal in his driveway and missed shots landed on his mother's car, past dirt roads we often turned down on cool October nights with only the dash light on our faces, rabbits fleeing in the headlights before us, past a landscape I watched every day for close to fifteen years on my way to and from school, the windows of the bus and the fields out the window all frosted over, like they are now, as we drive, past old weathered barns and old and new houses in changing landscape, past the house where I used to live, past rural country churches where the signs say "He is Risen" and "This is the day that the Lord hath made; Let us rejoice, and be glad in it."

The snow comes Christmas Day. Sleet in the early afternoon that soon turns to snow. By nightfall the roads are blanked out, grass and trees thick with snow. Under the snow, everything looks fine. The town lies quiet as a blanket. The lights come on all along the streets and the snow streaks through the streetlights in myriad prisms. Soft light falls from the windows of the houses, Christmas lights strung up under the eaves. Thin wires of smoke tether themselves to the chimneys down main street, where the old houses used to look rich, but now sag groundward. Still, the snow erases the past, negates the years of neglect around the windows of the houses, makes everything fine again, almost new. If you are driving, or walking through, if you squint your eyes or ignore the empty sockets of the abandoned houses, if you refuse to look for the husked-out shells where fire has wrought its damage when the chemicals got out of control, you can forget that something immense lurks beneath the surface here, something you only talk about in whispers, late at night, in full rooms with all the lights on.

Full dark I walk down the hill to my grandmother's house. The snow is three to four inches deep. My feet slide under me, the surface slick and suspicious. The church bell chimes the hour. Smoke from chimneys melts into the falling snow, disappearing into the night. I wonder if there will be fires. Wrapped in the cold and snow I walk, the wind blowing in my face, snow settling in my eyelashes and hair. The house grows closer. Inside there will be warmth and light and food and laughter, but for just a moment I wish to keep walking, to hold this silence, hold this place in my heart just a few minutes longer.

My stepfather did not know what was in the little plastic bags. My mother suspected, and called the police. Within minutes the drug enforcement officer for the county—a man I went to high school with—had arrived. When he heard the story he said it must have been a drop-off, and someone would be looking for it.

The next day he set up surveillance cameras in the trees and brush where the flashlight had been. He came every morning to check them. He told my parents he would keep watch. He told them not to worry.

A few days later the cameras took a picture of a man the police knew kicking through the weeds near where the flashlight had been. He was wanted in a county north of ours for drug manufacturing and distributing, but was long gone by the time the police got the camera. The local agent stopped by my parents' house to tell them the news. When he left, he told them to report anything suspicious they saw in the area. He said there was nothing else they could do.

Christmas night a house burns in an adjacent town. When we drive back to North Carolina, the ashes are still smoldering, melting the newly fallen snow.

COLD

No matter how well my stepfather banked the ashes when he left for work, the fire went out before my brother and I got home from school, and the house was cold. The bus would drop us off on a gray afternoon already turning dark, and we'd stand in the front yard hoping for smoke rising from the chimney. The lights were off in the house. The sun fell behind the blue hills. When we went inside, we stood before the fireplace holding out our hands for some sliver of warmth.

It seems that house was always cold. The summer heat could knock you senseless, suck all the air out of your breath, and in spring storms swirled up every evening, sending tornados spinning out into the lightning-struck night, but when I think of winter I remember the constant cold, the chill air that came down from Canada to frost the fields and sheath the trees in ice. Wind whistled in the chimney, and we huddled close to the fireplace for any warmth left lingering in the stones.

When even the stones had grown cold, my brother and I brought in wood. In the backyard the grass lay stiff with frost, the distant fields turned white. My brother grabbed the wheelbarrow and angled it toward the woodpile. Our stepfather would not keep wood near the house. He said termites got into the wood and would get into the house and eviscerate it, a word we didn't know. Empty, gutted. This was the same house our mother and father had once lived in together, and now we lived there with different furniture and a different father, a man who thought of things being eviscerated.

We stacked the wheelbarrow with as much wood as it could carry. My brother pushed while I walked alongside, trying to keep it steady. The front wheel was always half-deflated, and the wheelbarrow wobbled side to side. Often, going through the snow or maneuvering down the sidewalk steps, the wheelbarrow tilted over, and when it did my brother cursed the wheelbarrow and the wood and our stepfather and the cold.

We docked the wheelbarrow next to a small woodbox built into the back of the house near the chimney. I went inside and opened the woodbox door while my brother handed each quarter-split log to me. I stacked them next to the fireplace, and when we were finished my brother came inside, both of us rubbing our hands, wishing for warmth.

We weren't allowed to build a fire. Instead we waited, huddled in front of the fireplace while the stones rang cold and the wind came down the chimney to stir the ashes. Sometimes snow fell in the late afternoon as the dark came on and we watched out the window as the flakes covered the grass in the backyard. Sometimes the air hovered at freezing and the rain that came could not decide whether it wanted to be rain or snow, and so fell as something in between, either sleet that rattled the leaves or slush that stuck to the sidewalks.

When our mother and stepfather got home from work, sometimes when the stars were already out, our stepfather started the fire. My brother and mother and I crawled under blankets on the couch to warm ourselves while we watched. He started by scooping out the cold ashes and carefully dumping them in a steel bucket. (Later, it was my job to empty the bucket, and there grew in our yard, right next to the old well we didn't use anymore, a gray mound of spent ashes that eventually turned to gray dirt, and which I never fail to think of at funerals.) Once the cold ashes had been cleaned away, he broke the pine kindling into smaller and smaller pieces. Ash rose around him. When he finished with the fire my brother and I would be asked to sweep around the fireplace, to clean up all the ash and bits of broken wood. But for now we only watched as he wadded newspaper beneath the kindling and set fire to it, or else, if there were any smoldering coals left in the ashes, he gently blew them back to life, until the fire caught and he could lay on more wood, until the flames rose and spread warmth throughout the house.

Our house sat halfway up a small hill, surrounded by hundred-year-old live oaks. Behind the house the hill climbed into a stand of pines, and beyond the pines the hill crested and fell down to a thin stream. In front of the house, across the narrow county highway, pastureland spread out, dotted with orange ponds and brown cattle, and beyond the fields the hills turned blue with distance.

Our yard was terraced into two different levels, separated by stone walls. A tall hedge surrounded a semi-circular driveway, and the live oaks flanked the sidewalk in the front yard. When I was younger I thought it exotic, like an old English manor, or what I imagined one would look like. The hedges were full of secret tunnels and hiding spots. My brother and I each had a hole we burrowed into the hedge to hide our favorite toys, and which the other was not supposed to know about. The rock walls held lizards and spiders and snakes on warm summer afternoons. Concrete pedestals flanked the steps that led from the semi-circular driveway to the front yard, the kind of thing that might have held lion statuettes in a different country, in a different time. A small garage/workshop stood next to the house, and wisteria formed a canopy over the flagstone patio. In summer bumblebees and wasps hovered overhead. In winter the wisteria vines looked shriveled and dead. In the spring we found pale eggs in tiny nests, and the flowers smelled sweet all through the fall.

The house itself was small. My mother and father had bought it when I was an infant. It is the first house I can remember living in: the wisteria growing over the patio, the columns flanking the sidewalk steps, the live oaks offering shade in summer. After my mother and father divorced, we moved to a small rented house along a curving county highway. Other houses, all alike, crowded in close to ours.

My brother hated the new house; we both missed our old one. When my mother and stepfather married, they bought the old house and we moved back in. I was ten then, my brother eleven. Our stepfather wore a beard. His head seemed too big, his voice too deep. Both of us were scared of him, though we had no reason to be other than the fact that he wasn't our father. Since the divorce we had been growing wilder, doing whatever we wanted, but our stepfather had rules to follow, chores for us to do, a house to warm. My brother did not get along with him; I only tried because I remembered my mother sitting on the porch of our rented house many afternoons by herself, smoking cigarettes in the last light, wondering, I thought, how she had ended up here, barely thirty, already divorced, two young boys to take care of by herself.

When we first lived there my brother and I shared a tiny bedroom, and our parents took the other. When we moved back, my stepfather added a new room onto the back of the house, almost doubling its size. My brother and I got our own bedrooms then, but it took a long time for me to get used to the new room—it made the house feel different. My brother and I weren't allowed in our parents' bedroom, and, along with the strange man living in our house, everything, even the walls of the place where we lived, felt foreign, and cold.

When he was a child my grandfather lived in a house with no insulation. The walls were made of green wood, and as the wood aged, it shrank, leaving gaps in the wall through which wind and snow and rain came. Sometimes he woke with lines of snow across his many blankets, or rain leaking down through the layers. He lay in bed until he heard his father filling the woodstove, lighting the fire, until he could see the first flames flickering in the other room.

I never woke with snow covering me, but each night our fire died down to nothing, and the house grew cold. In the morning I'd lie in bed and watch my breath. Frost formed on the windows and hung in the trees. My bedroom window faced east, and the sun fell through the webs of frost in myriad prisms, spreading a pink glow on the wall, filling the room with light.

My stepfather rose before anyone else and built the fire: ashes into the steel bucket, the coals breathed back to life. He laid the kindling on, then the wood, until the heat pushed him back and he sat with the firelight on his face. When the fire grew strong my brother and I left our beds and ran to the living room to stand before the flames, turning front and back to warm ourselves.

Once we had warmed, we ran to our bedrooms and dressed quickly, then came back to the fire while our mother cooked breakfast. When the oven and gas burners warmed the kitchen, we traded the fire for the stove, eating with the oven door open until it was time for school. We walked down to the highway and stood shivering with our hands in our pockets, hopping from one foot to the other, trying to stay moving, to keep blood circulating. From the kitchen window our mother and stepfather looked out, sipping coffee in the warm house, smiling and waving, my brother not waving back.

Then the bus came, smoke and steam leaking from the exhaust, the windows frosted over. In the fields cows stood with their breath fanning the air before them as mist rose from the small orange ponds. The bus stopped before us in a stink of diesel exhaust, warm kerosene air flooding out. Our friends huddled together near the heating vents, little pockets of warmth in the cold bus, and when we had climbed on, the driver spun the wheel, guiding us through a cold world covered white, the trees brittle enough to snap. On our way to school, out windows with our names drawn in frost, we'd see limbs sheared from the broken trees by the snap of ice, and I'd think of all the wood being wasted that could be used to heat our house. I'd know that behind us my stepfather would even now be banking the ashes, trying to retain some heat for when we returned.

He searched constantly for wood. Each fall Saturday unshaven men pulled into our yard and dumped truckloads of poplar and pine and oak and ash. These were lukewarm October afternoons with the clouds racing overhead, but my stepfather seemed to think Arctic conditions were already swooping down on us. As we stacked the wood, he would calculate in his head how much we used each night, how much more we might need. Like all the older men I knew as a child, he watched the weather constantly, always eyeing what might be coming in from the west. Mostly it was storms we had to worry about, tornados and high winds and hail, but in winter the cold came and gave my stepfather another element to fret over.

If we did run out of wood in the winter, my stepfather and I walked over the hill behind our house, searching for sheared limbs and shattered trees. As I followed my stepfather into the woods over the hill, I carried a tiny chainsaw. My stepfather carried the big chainsaw, and an axe. It had snowed the night before, and the morning sun reflected off the snow. Tiny birds flitted and hopped on the crust of snow, and our boots crunched down to the frozen earth while our breath belled out before us.

Among the pines on top of the hill we sought out dead or dying trees. No need to cut the living, he told me, when there was plenty already gone. When he found one, he'd drag it out to a clearing and with my little chainsaw I would cut all the limbs and stack them for kindling while he sawed the trunk into sizeable chunks, which we then carried back to the house, making trips back into the woods all day, until our stack of firewood had been built back up.

It always seemed to me we had enough to last a dozen winters, but still he worried. While my mother warmed soup on the stove and warmed my face with her hands, he rebuilt the fire, and when he had finished he leaned back on his heels and smiled, admiring what he had done, while the rest of us crowded in, hungering for warmth.

My brother never came with us. His relationship with my stepfather, cool at first, had become as cold as the house. I do not know if my brother did not like him because he wasn't our real father or because they just did not take to one another or if there were reasons neither of them could define, but they often shouted at one another. After the shouting, my brother stormed to his room and slammed the door. He stayed in his room most of the time. My mother chain-smoked on the couch while my stepfather went to fiddle with the fire and I stood in the middle of the house listening to the fire gathering strength but still feeling cold. In his frustration my stepfather would build the fire high enough to blacken the chimney stones. Sparks rose like anger. The smoke curled into the living room and made the air hard to breathe. It burned in our lungs like something that had gotten inside us while we weren't paying attention. The fire snapped and popped until I thought my stepfather meant to burn down the house to finally chase away the cold that still lingered, years after he and my mother had married. He sat alone by the fire until it had calmed, staring at the flames, sweat running down his face, until the fire was no more than ashes he banked against the coming night.

Their relationship grew steadily worse. My brother was thirteen or fourteen, his voice deepening, acne sprouting on his forehead, and he had decided he would not be told what to do by this man who wasn't our real father. Since we had moved into the house their relationship had rotted like wood left out all winter. When our mother first brought this strange man to visit, my brother had decided to ignore him, but after the marriage he could no longer pretend our stepfather would go away. They walked past each other without speaking because any conversation could turn into shouting. It often did. I lay in bed some nights listening to them yell at each other, my room already growing cold, frost already forming on the windows. Waiting for the bus in the morning, my brother would watch him waving from the window, then turn and stare across the fields as if searching for something.

One October day, while we were unloading wood, my brother told our stepfather he wasn't going to help. My stepfather calmly informed my brother that he was, indeed, going to help, and my brother cursed him. The exchange went on for some time before they both lost their tempers and exploded into anger. I don't remember the exact chain of events. One moment I was stacking wood, or splitting it, seeing the little pieces fly everywhere. The next moment all the cracks and crevices of our inner lives had come to the surface and split apart.

My stepfather came scrambling out of the truck. He tackled my brother and held him on the ground. My stepfather was a big man, but he had always been gentle. Now he was red-faced, shouting. My brother shouted back, spit flying from his lips. I stood there thinking it the end of the world. My stepfather held my brother on the ground while my brother kicked and screamed. My stepfather was only trying to calm him, but it made my brother angrier. He kicked and screamed and cursed, and later that night, near midnight under a giant moon that seemed to swim outside my window like an angry face, I heard my parents' voices from the other room. I couldn't make out the words, but my stepfather's voice sounded weak and high-pitched—I thought he was near tears. I was too. We all were. We lived in a house that had once belonged to our mother and father and now we had moved back, but with a man who was supposed to be our new father. Everything the same, but different, as if most of our childhood was now being replaced. Our stepfather was also divorced—he had children from his first marriage that he rarely saw. He didn't mention them often, and it was many years later before I realized how difficult starting over in a new place must have been for him too. Like my mother, he was trying to begin again, to succeed where he had failed before. He had already lost one family, and now here he was with another, trying to hold it together with two boys who wanted nothing to do with him.

They stayed up talking for a long time. After the fight, my brother had disappeared into the woods behind our house, and had only come home after dark. For hours, before night fell, I had walked through the pine trees shouting for him, but heard nothing in response. By the time dark came, I thought he had disappeared forever. My stepfather must have thought so too.

The first fingers of frost webbed the window, spreading out like the cracks in the wood we split that afternoon. It was still October, but the nights had grown cold enough you did not want to get out of bed. You only wanted to pull the covers over your head as if you were still a small child, hiding from the cold that lingered in the darkness of a fractured house.

Thirty years later, near Christmas at a quiet bar in North Carolina after he and my mother had flown in to visit, I asked my stepfather what he'd been thinking, what he and my mother had talked about that night.

"I thought you and your brother hated me," he said.

For most of the time I lived with my stepfather in that house, before we all moved to a house in town, with a heating unit and a fireplace that we never used, one of my chores was to split wood. I hated it at first, but after a time began to enjoy the work, the way the smooth handle of the axe felt in my hands, the power I could call up when swinging it downward, the wood splitting beneath my stroke, the feeling that I was contributing to keeping the cold away. After the fight my brother and stepfather avoided one another for a time, hard to do in the small house, but after more time had gone they began slowly speaking to one another.

The house grew warmer, but I continued to chop wood. Every afternoon after school I swept the woods behind our house for fallen trees, then sliced them with the saw and split the logs and stacked it, the woodpile growing, me trying to shore up our meager supplies so that we might make it through another winter, when the cold came down and seemed to settle in with us there in the small house. I blackened fingernails and flattened thumbs, and even now, writing this, I wince at the remembered pain of cold fingers struck by a metal wedge, or a thumb accidentally smashed by a twelve-pound hammer on a cold November afternoon, but I kept working all through the fall and into the early winter.

I spent long hours in the side yard where we kept the wood, often alone, working until the first stars came out in the purple evening. My brother and stepfather were slowly coming to know one another, and the fights were fewer and further between. We had finally, after years of saving, gotten a fireplace insert, which made the fireplace more efficient, and lessened our need of wood, but I spent hours splitting wood anyway, falling into a rhythm of silent work, the sharp crack of the axe echoing in the evening air. I had gotten to be sixteen by then, and soon I would leave home for the Army, and then college, and then marriage after that. My brother was often gone, the house was warm, and on cold afternoons my stepfather would come work beside me, neither of us saying anything, just splitting log after log, stacking the split pieces, occasionally leaning on the handle of the axe to watch the shadows come together and night fall over the blue hills.

When the first cold nights came in and my stepfather started the first fires of winter, I went out to look at what we had gathered in the last light. The stacks of wood were high above of my head, running longer than the house, row after row, but I worried if it would be enough to last.

Six months before we moved to North Carolina a winter storm dropped three inches of ice across Western Arkansas and knocked out power to that part of the state. My older daughter was three, my younger daughter six months. We had no fireplace in the house, no way to stay warm, so my wife and I piled blankets on our bed and huddled together, the four of us, with a dozen candles lighting the room. Outside, the wind howled. All the streetlights were out, but the world glowed under a sharp moon, reflected by the ice covering everything. Trees lay everywhere. The roads were blanked out. Frost formed thick on the windows.

The next morning we were woken by a knock on the door. My stepfather stood outside. He had wrapped chains on his truck tires and driven over to get us. My wife and I bundled our daughters and threw on our coats and climbed in the truck. We drove through an empty world. All the stores were closed. We were the only car on the road. Fog rose from the little creeks we passed over. The trees lay sheathed in ice, and occasionally we saw limbs falling, crashing to the ground, breaking other limbs as they fell.

My stepfather drove us to my grandmother's house, where the rest of the family had gathered. There was no fireplace in her house, but the power had been restored on this side of town, and the heat was on. In the kitchen the oven ticked. Condensation clung to the windows. Steam rose from the heating vents like smoke. My grandmother stood by the glass door, watching for us. Behind her, we could see my aunts and uncles and cousins and mother. My brother was there too. My stepfather had gone to get him as well, driving an hour through the snow and ice. He held the door for us.

"Get inside," he said as we crossed the ice. "Warm yourselves."

OF LITTLE FAITH

My kindergarten teacher, Mrs. Denett, was pregnant the entire school year. She waddled down the narrow row between our desks, occasionally hitting someone in the eye with her extended womb. During nap time she put headphones on her stomach and we could faintly hear classical music drifting out, though none of us knew why she put them on her stomach and not her ears.

In first grade I had Mrs. Rankin, whose husband was a high school coach, and so underneath her perfumy smell was the faint odor of the Atomic Balm the track runners rubbed into their calves before the long jump or decathlon.

Mrs. McCarthy in second grade was old and doddering and occasionally lost her pencil in her hair, and the two Mrs. Bradys, my third and fourth grade teachers, attended square dances and hay-gathering events on their off-days.

But it was Mrs. Butler in fifth grade who taught us we were all going to Hell.

This was the rural South, the thick strap of the Bible Belt, near the buckle. Every morning our elementary school principal said a prayer over the intercom. Our school's daily flyer always listed a Bible verse of the day, and before any sporting event we bowed our heads and mumbled the Lord's Prayer. Those of us in my fifth-grade class already knew, from being dragged to church with our grandparents, that drinking and drugs and fornication started a slow spiral that led straight to the other place, but those were only the biggies, Mrs. Butler told us, the ones everyone knew to watch for. This was the first day of school, the ink not yet dry where we had signed our names in our textbooks, which, we were told, we would be reading very little from because non-Bible literature did not glorify God. She stood in front of the class tapping her teeth with a pencil, her name written in tight white cursive on the chalkboard behind her. The bell had just rung and outside it was still summer, heat shimmering from the sidewalks and already a fetid stink developing in the air from sweat and lack of deodorant.

"Satan," she said, "is everywhere," and then began a long list of things she considered unholy, such as the digital watches we wore, the rock-n-roll music we listened to, and our failure to say grace before drinking our pint cartons of chocolate milk at snack time.

When we weren't learning about Columbus bringing Christianity to the heathens in the New World or how America was founded on religious principles, we heard about the dangers of wrist wear, evil colors, devil worship, communism, and not having table manners. According to Mrs. Butler, yellow represented Satan, digital devices were banned in the Bible, and devil-worshippers were everywhere, probably in the big yellow house with the digital sign out front. The Soviet Union was full of atheist-communists, which we thought meant they lived in a commune and didn't bathe, but which Mrs. Butler told us meant they hated God and America and wanted to destroy us. Not saying grace was an invitation for demons to fly in your mouth while you were chewing. I think now it would have been a better argument for us to chew our food with our mouths closed than to say grace, but in fifth grade, we weren't taking any chances, so we did both.

Or most of us did—thirty years later, I'm sure Steve Garrison still chews his food with his mouth open.

Mrs. Butler went to one of the churches even the religious among us feared, a one-room Pentecostal with paint flaking from the steeple and a sign out front that always said "Repent" or "Judgment Day Is Upon Us" in straight black letters. None of us had ever been inside, but we'd all heard rumors of people flopping on the floor, speaking in fire and claiming tongues, visions of chariots and cherubs appearing in the air. We imagined the Sunday service lasting ten or twelve hours as the preacher—a small thin man with iron-gray hair plastered to his head—read long lists of the evil dangers loose in the world, his congregation nodding their heads and amening every few seconds as he listed hairspray, tomatoes, and books not written by an apostle as things to avoid in life. Every Monday Mrs. Butler came to school with a new list of evils to watch for: hoofed animals, cemeteries not on hallowed ground, meals containing eggplant.

Led by Mrs. Butler, we prayed both before and after the Pledge of Allegiance in the morning. She led our class in collaborative grace before we went single-file to the lunchroom, and then reminded us to say individual grace before we ate yesterday's meatloaf. When a boy in our class's father was injured at work, Mrs. Butler reminded us all to pray for him, and to pray for the boy, who took off his thick glasses and wiped at his eyes before running out the door when the bell rang. Perhaps we took it too far, but we began to pray before recess that no one would get hurt, and when someone did get hurt we prayed for his or her speedy recovery, that the Bactine would not sting too much, that the scab on his knee would heal quickly, that the Band-Aid would not stick to his skin. When storm clouds came threatening over the hills in the west, we prayed that tornadoes would not strike our town. When the lights went out we prayed they would come back on. We clasped hands as we hid under our desks during nuclear missile drills and prayed that everyone's life be spared, and when it was over: the storm, the missile warning, the trip to the nurse's office, we thanked God that everything had turned out fine in the end.

She wore black horn-rimmed glasses that actually looked like horns where they framed her short black hair. She always wore a grayish sweater and wool skirt that made someone in the class sneeze. It might have been the girl who was a Jehovah's Witness, and Mrs. Butler might have worn them on purpose, although it's possible I am just being vindictive. But it's strange to me now to still be thinking about her. She was about as old as I am now, which doesn't seem real, and some days her sweater was as gray as the rain, and her face under the flickering fluorescent lights as gray as the weather, and we almost felt sorry for her as she stared out the window while we wrote in our journals, until she reminded us that country music, which our parents listened to, was just as bad as rock-n-roll, although in a less Satan-worshippy way.

When she began her long lists of the sin afflicting our world, we were forced to think of the immoral things our parents did: drinking, smoking, the sex we knew went on from the late-night sounds vibrating the walls of our houses, the quickening pulse of bedsprings. My parents went to church on Easter and Christmas, and rarely any other time, which made me wonder, after a few months with Mrs. Butler, about their immortal souls, and mine, and where we would end up when a storm finally flattened the town or frogs fell from the sky like the book of Revelations tells us will happen. Down the road from my house stood a Baptist church, where the preacher said some of the same things Mrs. Butler did, and we began to wonder what was right and wrong in this world. We knew from the Ten Commandments written on the court-house lawn that killing was wrong, and adultery, and worshipping carved statues, but we never knew, at that age, where to draw the line. If carved statues were evil then maybe yellow was too. Working on Sunday was evil, but what if the calendar had been messed up at some point and Sunday was actually Friday? And what exactly did honoring thy father and mother mean? Were we supposed to carve images of them? Was it adultery to hold hands with two girls in one recess? Was it stealing if you meant to give something you had stolen back after you had grown tired of it?

She warned us of wristwatches and prime colors because she knew, she said, how easy it was for Satan to get inside you, which always made me think of the movie *Alien* and that thing that comes spitting out of the man's stomach. Every action we performed had an inherent danger attached to it, either for our bodies or our souls. We could walk out the door and get hit by a snowmobile or be abducted into a yellow-worshipping cult, and then where would we be, Mrs. Butler seemed to ask—where would we end up?

As August swept into September we began to see the long year ahead of us. We had to pray before being let out to recess, a prayer led by Mrs. Butler, where she would ask the Lord to watch over us, and protect us from spinal injury, broken teeth, collapsed lungs, punctured spleens, pierced eyes, or anything she worried might happen to us while we played touch football or TV tag. She started off each day with another Bible verse after the school-approved prayer and Bible verse, and ended each day by reading from Matthew, Mark, Luke, or John, and sometimes, while we wrote in our journals, our finger-paintings drying on the walls, we'd raise our heads to see her sitting at her desk, reading from a Bible with her initials emblazoned on the cover, her jaw silently working. Out the window we could see the recess fields, with volleyball net and assorted jungle gym equipment, the soccer field gone muddy now with fall rains, the streets surrounding the school, the houses beyond that. Above the houses rose the water towers with the name of the town painted in big high letters, and in the other direction we could just see the spires of the Baptist church and the Methodist church, across the street from one another at the center of town, signboards out front reading "God Forgives," and "There is one place hotter than Arkansas."

In early October she began intoning her hatred for Halloween. Our school year was divided by the holidays, preparing for Halloween giving way to preparing for Thanksgiving and Christmas. In our journals we wrote "What Halloween Means to Me" and Mrs. Butler admonished us not to forget the Lord in anything we said or did or wrote. Halloween, she said, was a time to reflect on Hell and the torment that awaited us there, not to stuff our faces with fake orange peanuts and chocolate vampires. It glorified witches and werewolves, she told us, ghosts and ghouls and goblins, demons and doppelgangers. All were agents of Satan. Costumes were evil, because once you put on the skin of a witch or a warlock, it was far too easy, she admonished, to become one. She warned us to dress as doctors and nurses, cowboys and cowgirls, and whatever we did, not to accept food from strangers, for razor blades lurked in every apple, and poison in every peanut butter cup.

Thanksgiving was a pagan harvest ritual, and people would do best to remember that. It was God who founded this country through the Puritans, she said, and it was God we needed to give thanks to, not Indians.

Christmas, we would learn, was under attack. Look at the commercialism! she would rail. Look at the symbolism! Where's Jesus in all this? Santa is just a few rearranged letters from Satan! Or Stan! She reminded us that we should not be celebrating with presents and pagan trees, but the birth of Christ, our savior and messiah, without whom we would have no reason for living, and I am reminded now how fiercely some people need to cling to a reason for living, the strange sadness that sometimes comes up on us that we actually need a reason—whether internal or eternal—to keep us going.

Of course we thought her strange. No one could possibly have a problem with Halloween. No one could equate the color yellow with evil. No one could actually believe music was inherently wrong, that certain types of rhythms might inspire Satan to rise up through the tiled floors of A. R. Hederick Elementary School and drag us screaming down to Hell. But when the principal, a huge man with huge hands and a red-veined nose, who kept an "electric" paddle in his office, reads verses from Revelations every morning over the loudspeaker, you tend to accept that evil lurks in the world, and you might want to be looking out for it.

I've often wondered why she was never fired. But this was the breadbasket of the Religious Right, where tornadoes wiped out towns every spring and the sirens lit up the night so we could all practice what to do if Soviet missiles ever launched toward us. The conservative '80s had not yet changed to the perhaps-slightly-more-liberal '90s, and it seemed no one was upset enough at the non-separation of church and state to complain to the school board. I imagined faceless men in gray suits hearing the rumblings of unease at what she preached in the classroom, but always they folded their hands and grunted and decided to let it be, thinking fear and worship a good thing in children in a changing world, and so we sat silently, trying to sleep while she read "The Parable of the Prodigal Son," trying to ignore the constant prayer, the stories of sin and death, fire and brimstone, the listing of the evils at loose in the world in the form of Judas Priest and Dungeons and Dragons and the visible light spectrum, the way the constant worry made us feel. Firing her would have saved generations of fifth-grade students from her opinions of evil snare drums and paintbrushes, from fear for their mortal souls, but that didn't happen, or, if it did, happened much later, and year after year students were forced to listen to her read from Genesis the story of God creating the world, of Adam and Eve and the serpent, the naming of rivers and beasts, Cain and Abel, not stopping until it was time for recess. After recess there would be all the begats and how old the oldest old men were, all the way up to Noah and God destroying the world because of its evilness, before the day ended and they went home to their small houses with the sad crocheted doilies and signs reading "Bless This Mess."

On the last day of school several of us decided we were going to tell Mrs. Butler off. We'd swirl our index fingers around our ears and then point at her. We'd tell her we loved the color yellow. We'd proudly hold up our wristwatches and proclaim our love for rock-n-roll. We wanted her to know she'd made us feel scared and uncertain and small, and telling her she was crazy was our way of extracting revenge for forcing us to see evil lurking everywhere in the world, and to live in constant fear, finding comfort only in words offered while kneeling, whispered under our breath like children with the covers pulled over our heads.

But as we waited to walk out the door that last day thirty years ago, and we could see the sunlight beyond the doorway, Mrs. Butler took off her glasses to clean them on her shirt. She looked up for a moment, blinking her weak eyes, and we said nothing. Just stood waiting to leave. She put her glasses back on and we filed out of the class and into the rest of our lives. Mrs. Butler stood at the door, looking out for all of us one last time, offering her form of protection against all the things in the world we might encounter, saying "God bless you, God bless you, God loves you" as we walked by.

STORM COUNTRY

⁂

When the storms came in the spring, we went underground. This was Western Arkansas, not far from the Oklahoma line, and all afternoon, as the radio gave reports of thunderstorms marching east across the windblown prairie, my father would alternate between listening to the radio and watching the sky, the radio braying static in the flashes of lightning. My mother opened windows, worrying about the curtains. My brother and I got out candles, a flashlight in case the power went out. Outside, the air was heavy and still, the leaves on the trees listlessly hanging as the storm moved closer and the nasal voice on the radio told of a line of severe storms from Tulsa to Muskogee, moving east at thirty-five miles per hour, bringing high winds and hail, lightning, the possibility of tornadoes. My father would go outside and stand in the yard, scanning the western horizon, and at some point, usually when the first black clouds appeared over the purple hills, or even earlier, when the late afternoon light looked like it was seen through yellow glass, my father would snap off the radio.

"Let's go," he would say, and we would rush out through the beginning rain or an unusually warm afternoon or a hot night lit up by lightning, coloring the world white so that the darkness seemed greater when it returned. The trees swayed in a hostile wind, brown grasses rippling out across the fields. Leaves and branches and scraps of paper lifted in the wind, hovering in air. My father held me tight to his chest, one hand on the back of my head as we climbed in his truck and drove up the hill to my grandfather's house, where the men of my family gathered outside the storm cellar. When they saw us coming up the road they rushed to the truck, taking my brother and me, ushering my mother inside, out of the wind and rain. My father would stay outside, accept a cup of coffee and a cigarette, join the other men in keeping an eye on the developing storm.

The cellar was built away from the house, a small structure of cinderblocks about the size of an outhouse. The door stood upright, opening on a sharp descent of concrete steps that were always crossed by spiderwebs that would wrap around my face as I hurried down. A small window was cut into the cinderblocks just above ground level, so you could walk a few steps down the stairs and still see what was forming in the air outside.

Inside, the cellar smelled of damp and earth. While my father and uncles and grandfather watched the storm, my mother herded my brother and me down the stairs where, in a little room at the bottom, my grandmother and aunts and cousins sat quietly in the light of a kerosene lamp, their shadows thrown large on the wall. Their eyes were dark and silent. In the room there were only four cots with damp quilts and a small table holding the kerosene lamp, a 12-volt flashlight, some candles, and the Bible. Outside, the storm was gathering strength, and to quiet the children, my grandmother would tell stories, or sing songs in a deep voice, and only occasionally would her eyes flicker to the door. Late at night, if the storm was a long one, or if we'd been woken up in the middle of the night and torn from our beds to be taken to the cellar, my brother and I would fall asleep in our mother's lap, closing our eyes to the movement of shadows on the wall, soft voices above the sound of the wind and rain outside telling us all was safe.

Sometimes I'd stand near the door at the bottom of the stairs, peeking through the crack and craning my head up to watch my father. When the rain and wind hit, the men would step inside the door. They'd stay on the stairs, though, instead of coming down, watching the storm through the window cut at ground level for that purpose. They smelled of coffee and cigarettes and the rain that sometimes blew in the little window if it was opened to hear the storm better. Sometimes they nodded toward a cloud off over the hills that might uncoil at any moment into a tornado. They scanned the skies, judging the weather, when it might be safe to return home.

Throughout the evening the radio would give reports, telling where tornadoes had touched down and where power lines had fallen and where golf-ball sized hail had been seen. Sometimes the radio reported that the storms were losing intensity, or that they had all moved through and passed on, and sometimes we slept in the cellar, waking up in the morning to the smell of molding quilts and kerosene, climbing the stairs to emerge into a bright world after the storms had passed, the spring grass glistening with the rain from the night and all around leaves and branches and debris from the storm littering the ground. We'd climb in the truck and drive around, surveying the damage. Sometimes trees would be blocking the road, or an old barn would have fallen from the wind. Sometimes there'd be hail covering the ground as if it had snowed, and as the day warmed the hail would steam as it evaporated, a low mist hanging over the fields.

Other times there would be no sign that any storm had ever come through but for a light rain that patterned the dirt, but when we got home and watched the news we would learn that the next town over had been hit, that people were dead and homes were destroyed, that anyone wishing to donate food or clothing or blood could call this number on the screen. On these days I'd walk out under the clear sky, trying to recall the night in the cellar, the way it smelled and felt and tasted, the way the storm looked when it passed, at what point the men decided it was over. After the storms I always felt unmoored and adrift, as if something had passed that I didn't quite understand.

In March in Arkansas the Gulf Stream sucks up moisture from the Gulf of Mexico to collide with cold air from up north, lingering remnants of winter meeting the warmth of spring. The clash of opposite air masses sends lines of tornadoes spinning out over the prairies of Kansas and Oklahoma and Texas, into the hills of Arkansas. In the late afternoon, they color the day like an old sepia photograph as they roll in, shading the light. At night, you can see funnel clouds in the flashes of lightning, or low-hanging spikes from which—my father would tell me as I got older—tornadoes could spawn.

Long before storm-chasing became an excursion for the rich or fool-hearted, my father and grandfather watched tornadoes from the stairs of our cellar, judging when they might drop, how big they might be, if we were in danger. They judged clouds as some men judge the stock-market, wondering if it might rise or fall, as all through spring and into summer the storms in Tornado Alley rolled up out of the west, advancing in lines extending from thirty miles south of Broken Bow, Oklahoma, to fifteen miles north of De Queen, Arkansas. I learned the counties of Arkansas—Logan and Sequoia and Crawford and Sebastian and Scott, Franklin and Johnson and Washington and Pope and Polk—through radio reports of tornado warnings or sightings, my geography formed of radio static in lightning, late nights in a storm cellar. I learned to judge the movement of storms across a TV screen, how a storm moving north-north-east through Scott County might end up in my own Logan, or how long it might take a tornado in Sebastian County to reach my house if it were moving at thirty-five miles an hour. I learned to recognize at a glance my own county and the counties surrounding it, the way, when tornado watches or warnings have been issued, in the bottom right part of the TV screen would be a map of Arkansas with certain counties flashing red. On these nights I lay awake in bed, red bands of heavy storms moving across computer-drawn counties in my mind, reciting the path of storms: LeFlore, Sebastian, Crawford, Logan, knowing that at some time in the night I would be awakened, either by my father or the storm outside. I would be wrapped in a blanket, hurried through the rain and into the truck and up the hill, to the flickering kerosene images of aunts and cousins, sleepy-eyed like myself, their shadows large on the wall, as outside the storm raged on.

My grandfather could tell by the way leaves hung on the trees if it would rain that day or not—an old-time meteorologist who watched the seasons and the sky simply because they were there.

"See there?" he said once. We were standing outside the cellar as the first storms began to fire up in the heat of late afternoon. Low green clouds hung silent in the distance, and I since learned that when clouds turn green, take cover. A point hung from the cloud, a barb that looked ominous as the clouds passed on and we watched them go, and always after I have looked for low barbs hanging from dark green clouds, for silent formations that might spawn destruction. He knew, standing on the cellar stairs watching through the little window, when a tornado might drop from the clouds. He knew the feel of the air, the presence that announces a heavy storm.

Sometimes it will stop raining when the funnel falls. Sometimes the wind stops and the trees go still and the air settles on you as everything goes quiet. Then, faint at first as the storm gathers speed, you can hear the force as it spins itself into existence, touching earth, whirling out into the day or night. It sounds like rusted sirens, howling dogs, the call of a freight train on a long trip across the plains somewhere in the western night, pushing speed and sound before it, lonely and forlorn on its midnight ride.

I've seen tornadoes drop from a clear blue sky. I've seen barns and houses and fields wiped out, cattle thrown for a distance to lie in the rain bawling with broken legs. Once I watched as a three- or four-hundred-pound cut of sheet metal floated across the highway, touched down once, then lifted off again, light as air. I've seen towns wrecked by tornadoes in November, houses swept away, all that was left of a church the roof lying on the ground, unscathed but for a few shingles missing at one corner. One time I was almost struck by a bullet of hail the size of my fist. It crashed through the window and landed on our living room floor. We all looked at it for a moment. My mother tried to protect the curtains as the rain came in, but my father herded us toward the cellar up the hill at my grandfather's house.

I know the sound of storms, the low growl of thunder that means storms in the distance, the loud quick clap that means storms overheard. I've blinked in the afterglow of forked lightning, watched flash lightning light the hills as night turns into day. I've seen the remains of exploded houses, nothing left of the house but kindling, from when the tornado drops and the air pressure changes and the air inside the house has to get out.

I've seen storms come with no warning, boiling up out of a western sky rimmed with the red rays of the last sun, lightning flickering in the twilight, the air gone heavy and still. I've seen them sweep through with hardly a ripple but the wind in your hair, passing to other places and other times. I've huddled in hallways and bathtubs and cellars listening to tornadoes pass overhead, and when I see on television the remnants of a town destroyed by the force of storms, I always offer, however briefly, a thanks that it was not my people, nor my town.

The first tornado I can remember was when I was eight. The storm came in the afternoon, as many storms do. It was early

March, a month that, as the saying in Arkansas goes, enters like a lion, leaves like a lion. My father was watching a basketball game on TV when the sound disappeared, followed by the steady beep that means an announcement is coming. Thunderstorms are moving through the area, the announcement ran at the bottom of the screen. Tornadoes possible. Take shelter. When the announcement disappeared the state of Arkansas appeared on the screen, the western counties lit like radiation. My father went out to study the sky and came back in at a run.

"Let's go," he said.

The trees were dancing as we ran to the truck, leaves and small branches swirling in the wind and falling all around. At the road up the hill to my grandfather's house a dust devil danced before my father ran his truck through it. A line of rain moved toward us through the fields. The clouds in the distance were green.

By the time we reached the top of the hill the wind was rocking the truck and the first drops of rain were hitting the hood, big and loud and hard. The curtain of rain reached us, going from a few drops to a downpour in an instant. The wind ripped the truck door from my father's hand. My grandfather ran out from the cellar door, where he'd been watching for us. He took my brother, my father took me. We couldn't see the cellar in the rain. Thunder rumbled the hills, and lightning stabbed down, sharp and quick, splitting the rain, everything quiet for an instant before the thunder struck.

We splashed through the rain and into the cellar. I was wet, plastered to my father's chest. My mother took us down the stairs. My father and grandfather stood peering through the window at the rain. The day had gone dark.

Downstairs, my grandmother was telling stories to my two younger cousins, who were flinching in the sharp crashes of each thunder. The room smelled of kerosene, of earth and wind and rain. My skin was wet, hair cold as my mother wrapped me in a quilt. In the brief silences between thunderclaps, we could hear the rain and my father and grandfather on the stairs. I peered through the door and heard my father say, "There it is."

He turned and saw me standing at the bottom of the stairs and motioned me up. The rain had slowed and was falling lightly now, the wind settled down in the trees. I stood on the steps with my father as he pointed in the distance, where a dark funnel coiled downward from the black clouds, like smoke, or wind taking shape and color. At the base of the tornado dust and debris hovered, circling slowly, and I heard the sound of storm for the first time. It grew out of air, out of wind. It seemed as silent as noise can be, a faint howling that reached us over the rain, almost peaceful from a distance. But then it would hit a line of trees, or a fence, shooting trees and fence posts and barbed wire into the air. It crossed over a pond and water turned it almost white for an instant. It hit an old barn like a fist, smashing boards and metal, slinging the debris about.

We watched, not speaking, as the tornado moved over the empty fields in the distance, leaving a swath of devastation in its wake. After a time it folded itself back into the underbelly of the clouds, rising silently, dispersing like smoke in the wind, the sound gone and the air still once again.

"It's over," my father said, but I could still see in my mind the black funnel dropping from the clouds, twisting across the landscape, throwing trees and dirt and anything in its path, tearing tracts of land as it went on its way. Before me was the result, the path of the tornado, cut through the hills. And, for no reason it seemed, it faded away, gone as surely as it had come.

We stood there for a long time after it was over, silent, watching the clouds roll on through, speeding swiftly toward night. After a time—an hour or three or four—the clouds peeled back, revealing bright stars flung across the sky.

My father, and my grandfather, must have watched other tornadoes before, just like that one, had seen them and knew what they could do. I had thought that they were standing guard through the night, watching until it was safe for us to come out, putting themselves between us and the danger that lurked outside. But as we turned and went down the stairs together I realized they watched from the window to see the terrible beauty of the storm rolling across the hills, hail falling from the sky, streaks of lightning in the jagged edges of the storm, the twisting funnel of clouds that held such power.

GIRL ON THE
THIRD FLOOR

The upper floors of the Nyberg Building are locked and deserted now, but her ghost is said to live there still. It is not hard to imagine a ghost filtering down the long hall and disappearing into the distance, although I do not know if she walks through walls or simply appears and stands looking sad and lost, perhaps trying to find someone to help her.

The Nyberg is part of the Human Development Center, a cluster of buildings whose construction began in 1910, in the hills of Arkansas, as a tuberculosis sanatorium, which was later converted, in the 1970s, to a home for the developmentally disabled. Those who live near the Center, or have worked there, tell tales of phantom lights in the buildings at night, strange noises, pockets of cold on the upper floors. Almost nothing is known of the girl's origins, not her name or age or when she lived there, not the reason people began to believe in her ghost in the first place. Yet the stories of her persist, stories I heard as a child living in a rented house on the grounds of the Center, only a short walk from the Nyberg. Paranormal groups have visited over the years and left toys for the girl: a writing tablet with the word *Hello* and a smiley face drawn on it; a once-white teddy bear that has grown brown with dust;

a stuffed tiger missing one eye. In the late '70s the building was cleared of asbestos, and the ceilings are open to rafters and pipes. Electrical cords hang down like vines, or vipers. The halls drip with heat. Dust hangs in the air, coats the floors and windows. On the higher floors dead birds line the hallways like stones, having been unable to find their way out once they got in. In this way they are like the tuberculosis patients, many of whom called the Nyberg their final home. Their presence lingers. It is hard to breathe inside the building, and though I know it is the dust and heat, I imagine tuberculosis hanging like the motes in shafts of light or the spirits of those who once lived here. There are more than a dozen other buildings among the pines at the Human Development Center, most of them boarded over now. If there are such things as ghosts, they would come here. I tell myself I do not believe in ghosts, but the Nyberg is a strange, sad place.

I came in mid-summer, driving south from Booneville through a browned pasture, across an orange river, and up a winding hill where the road curved around ridges that looked out on other hills blue with distance. Past a final curve the Center rose through a forest of pine. From far away the buildings looked bone-white, but up close were nearer the color of old dirt. Bradford pears lined the sidewalks. The manicured lawn, and the dorm-like buildings among the rows of pines, looked more like a college campus than an old sanatorium.

I had not come to look for ghosts, except for the ones I already knew. My mother worked here for most of her adult life, and for three years we lived in one of the small houses on the grounds. That was just after my parents divorced, and the house seemed empty without my father there. Every morning my brother and I walked through the long shadows thrown by the buildings to catch the school bus, and every afternoon crossed back again, avoiding the residents, whose strange faces and various afflictions unnerved us. Many of them had speech impediments, and could not form words correctly, so it often seemed they were grunting, or yelling. Some nights, when all the buildings turned dark and the voices of the grunting or yelling residents drifted over the grounds, my brother and I crept out of our house and slipped through the trees to climb the water towers or crawl through broken windows into abandoned buildings. We sneaked into the old chapel and the fire station and peered into the steam tunnels that ran beneath the buildings.

Until today, I had not been back in twenty years.

Nor had I ever been on the upper floors of the Nyberg, though as a boy I walked in its shadow every morning for three years and saw it lit up at night from my bedroom window. Even after we moved back into the town below the hill I would watch it rise from the mountaintop. For over twenty years, until I left Arkansas for North Carolina, it was a part of the landscape, an indelible reminder of the past. I could not look at it without some memory filtering in.

The first tuberculosis sanatorium opened in Poland in 1863. About twenty years later the Saranac Lake, New York, sanatorium became the first North American facility. In the early 1900s, the dry climate of Arizona drew many suffering from tuberculosis, among them several Arkansas state senators who petitioned the state for money to build the sanatorium. While wintering in Arizona to "take the cure," as it was called, they realized few people in their home state had the means to travel to Arizona.

Construction began in 1910, after Act 378 approved the establishment of the Arkansas State Tuberculosis Sanatorium, and the town of Booneville donated 970 acres atop Potts Hill. At first there was only a twenty-four-bed hospital along with a few outbuildings, but the sanatorium grew with the spread of the disease. For the next thirty years, new buildings were added, including a dairy farm, employee cottages, and a water-treatment facility so that the sanatorium could run self-sufficiently.

The prescribed treatment for tuberculosis was rest and food. The pines and clear air were thought to be an expedient for cure, but during the '20s and '30s doctors began experimenting with treatments. They collapsed patients' lungs and filled the cavity with ping-pong balls to give the lungs a rest. The phrenic nerve—the long cord that connects the spinal column to the diaphragm—was removed from some patients. There was a farm on the grounds that raised guinea pigs for drug testing.

When the Nyberg Building was completed in 1941, a few months before the attack on Pearl Harbor, it was one of the largest tuberculosis hospitals in the world. The Nyberg held an X-ray laboratory, infirmary, morgue, and 501 patient beds. It was a tenth of a mile long and fifty feet wide, standing among the surrounding pine trees like an undiscovered city or an old monument carved to forgotten gods. Years of water damage have stained the sandstone bricks, and the granite etching over the doors has faded to a color closer to white than gray.

I parked and got out and craned my neck up at the building. It looked more like a prison than a hospital. I wondered how many of the people who had lived there over the years had thought that same thing. There are bars on the windows of the fifth floor, where criminals with tuberculosis were housed. Some of the rooms are made entirely of glass, designed such that the prisoners could be watched at all times. Those doors were locked from the outside.

Although I could find no evidence of who the girl was or how old she had been, I imagine her to be ten or eleven, about the age my younger daughter is now, about the age I was when I lived there. I picture her with brown hair, glasses, a way of looking out of the corners of her eyes as she twirls a strand of hair around her finger. Old newspaper reports and patient journals provide a way to reconstruct how she might have arrived there and what it must have been like to become trapped in such a place, in such a way.

It would have started with a cough, a dry rattle that shook her shoulders and made her parents exchange worried looks, until the day she began to cough blood. They lived on a dusty road in the middle of soy fields in the middle of the state in the middle of the country and one day a long black car pulled up in front of the house amid a cloud of dust that settled on the long rows of crops. A nurse got out. The girl's mother stood in the doorway. Her father, unable to watch it happen, went out the back door and through the rows of crops, not looking back, not seeing his only daughter put in the black car with the nurse's hands in the small of her back to guide her. He did not see the door shut, or the car pull away.

The windows were down and the hot air rushed in as they drove through the fields. When they turned onto the highway the droning engine put her to sleep. When she woke they were somewhere she had never been. She saw the buildings and the pines and asked where they were, how long she would be here, when she could go home. The nurse said to hush now, her voice softer than her face. She rubbed the girl's back and told her it would be all right.

The car drove through the pine trees in alternating shadow. Far down the mountain she could see an orange river, cow pastures spreading out in the distance, a town beyond the pastures. The pines stirred in the wind. Crickets were out in midday, their noise echoing among the pines. The car stopped in front of the Nyberg Building, still shiny and new. Inside, it was cool and dark. The nurse led her to a room on the third floor so small she could hardly turn around in it. A cracked washbasin sat on a nightstand beside a bed with iron springs and a thin mattress stained in places. A window looked out on other buildings. She sat down on the bed and waited.

The first floor of the Nyberg had been rebuilt, I saw as I opened the doors. The tile floors were buffed and polished. Modern air conditioners hummed and dripped condensation.

Wasps hovered outside the windows. The offices on the first floor were full of light, and cool after the summer heat.

I stood in a doorway for a few minutes until a woman at a desk noticed me. I told her who I was and why I was there and she picked up the phone and a man with a set of keys appeared a few minutes later. He told me his name and that he had worked there for close to thirty years. It turned out he had known my mother. Whether he agreed to take me on the tour because of that, or because it was a common request here, I didn't know.

From the first floor to the second we traveled fifty years into the past. Old movie posters from the '40s and '50s lined the wall in the stairwell, famous faces staring at us with eyes bright and happy, at odds with the feel of the place. The stairwell was gloomy, the light stained by the dirty window. There was no electricity, only the distant sounds of the building settling.

At the second-floor landing he pulled out the key ring again and unlocked the door and held it open for me. The sun came through a window at each end of the long hallway so that it seemed the hall disappeared into sunlight, like the tunnel reported by people who have near-death experiences. The floors had once been black and white in diamond patterns, but now all the tiles looked gray, hazed with time. Our feet left prints behind us. All the rooms were small, half the size of a college-dorm room, wide enough only for one or two narrow beds. Paint curled from the walls like dead skin. The baseboards had fallen away and the heat emanated from the walls and it was easy to believe theories of places becoming haunted by what they had once held within them.

On the third floor I saw the toys as we stepped out of the stairwell. The teddy bear sat atop a radiator. The writing pad—one of the plastic toy kinds that you can wipe with a hand to remove what you have a written—leaned against the wall. The toys were only a few years old, at odds with the antiquity of the place. The last patients here left in 1973, after antibiotics had virtually wiped out tuberculosis. The buildings were handed over to the State Board of Mental Retardation and the sanatorium was reborn as the Human Development Center. The upper floors of the Nyberg were closed then, and the rooms have not been occupied since.

When I asked about the toys my guide told me what he knew of the little girl, which wasn't much, other than that people over the years had begun to believe in her existence. Strange lights seen at night were attributed to her, as were ghostly noises people heard. There had been a children's ward in the building, and though he did not know the number of children who had died here or even if she had been a patient, I suspect the idea of a child's ghost walking the long halls began in an era of sadness and continues to this day. He told me there were always rumors here, stories of ghosts, of things that could not be explained. But perhaps there are always rumors, stories, histories of any place where people suffered and died, any place where days were measured in increments as tiny as breaths, and years passed as slowly as the sun moved across the floors of the small rooms.

When I asked him if he believed in ghosts he shook his head. He told me the lights people saw in the upper floors were the flashlights of the maintenance men performing safety checks, or searching for a forgotten piece of equipment (much of the place serves as storage now). He said the noises were nothing more than wind through the gaps in the roof or the cracks in a window or simply an old building settling and ticking like a warm house late at night while everyone is trying to sleep.

When I asked him if he believed the ghost of a girl lived here, he deflected the question by telling me several paranormal groups had toured the place recently with cameras and EVP equipment and lights and other electronic devices. They didn't find anything, he said.

When I asked why they were let in, he shrugged. "What's it going to hurt?" he said.

As we walked the length of the third floor I saw other toys: a small boat, colored pencils and paper, sidewalk chalk. I suppose those who left the writing utensils wanted the girl

to prove her existence somehow, which isn't much different than what I was doing. In the new paranormal shows
on TV, groups wander the halls of old asylums or prisons or
houses where murders have taken place or people have died
of strange causes. They shout things like "Show yourself" and
"Are you here?" and "Do you want to hurt me?" They never
ask, "Are you okay?" or "Do you want to go home?"

There are other ghosts at the Center.

When I lived there the voices of the residents would drift
through the buildings and down the hill on summer evenings,
our windows open to catch the breeze, and more than once I
woke sure that someone had been watching me through the
window. My mother told me sometimes the residents got out
at night and wandered through the trees, trying to find their
way home, wherever they had been before they came here,
and sometimes they got lost and had to call out for help.

The row of houses where I once lived is mostly deserted
now, and the houses themselves have turned to ghosts. A few
had always stood empty as people moved from one part of
their life to the next, but now leaves gather on the porches
in fall and winter and the yards are strewn with pine needles. The houses are old, and fewer people work at the Center,
and even fewer of those who do wish to live on the Center
grounds in houses almost as run-down as the boarded-over
buildings. Doors to the crawl spaces beneath the houses hang
open, and the front steps slant askew. There are no cars out
front of most of the houses, no bicycles in the front yard. The
windows are dusty and hazy, and some are broken, with dark
stars punched into them. They have taken on the abandoned
look houses acquire after standing empty for a time.

Across a narrow road from the houses, carved stones among
the pine trees mark the resting places of dead pets. When the
houses were all occupied, children chased each other through
the pines and hid and sought each other under the porches and
in the crawl spaces and sometimes crossed the road solemnly

to bury goldfish and hamsters and kittens hit by cars. Deep in the woods a small dam spans a narrow creek. The pool at the bottom of the dam is filled with old coins people have tossed in over the years, closing their eyes and wishing they were somewhere else, where the old buildings did not loom over them at night. The pine trees hold old names carved in wood and thickened now with sap, like bugs trapped in amber.

Other ghosts, the state senators who petitioned the state for money to build the sanatorium, live in the faded pictures that line the hallway on the first floor of the Nyberg. The buildings carry their names carved in stone. It is a policy of the institution that no building bear the name of a living person. Leo Nyberg, after whom the largest building is named, died of tuberculosis four months before it was completed.

According to the pamphlet *Tuberculosis or Consumption: Its Prevention and Treatment,* printed in 1925 by the Arkansas Tuberculosis Sanatorium, this would have been her day:

She woke at seven, drank a glass of hot water and sponged herself off, then walked up the hill to the commons building for breakfast. I like to think she sat with others her age, and I like to think they talked about boys sitting at a table nearby or dresses or dolls or anything girls like to talk about that isn't death and disease and the feeling of being trapped.

After breakfast they rested until first lunch at ten. Lunch consisted of milk and eggs, an old treatment used since the eleventh century to combat the emaciation that often accompanies tuberculosis. After first lunch she rested again until second lunch, two hours later. They rested in the hope that the tubercles would not spread, and that the lungs would wall off the offending areas and fight them, and they ate so much to give the body the strength to do the fighting.

After second lunch they rested outdoors. I prefer to think of children running and chasing one another, but the rules specified the rest was to be lying down, or reclining in special chairs. At six they ate again, then another hour of rest, then more food, then bed. I imagine her sitting long hours with her elbows on the windowsill, looking out at the pines, the hills receding into the distance.

In spring the storms came. Water ran down the window, and she flinched each time thunder rumbled. The air smelled of burnt ozone from the lightning strikes, and the town below the hill seemed underwater, as if the seas had risen once again and swallowed up the world and only those atop the mountain still lived.

In summer the heat grew fierce. She lay sweating on her bed in the mornings, counting the cracks in the ceiling, listening to the flies drone in the corners of the room. When she slept she dreamed of the house, the long rows of crops, her father's footsteps moving across the sagging floors, but when she opened her eyes it was the nurse's shoes on the tile floor that she heard.

In fall she watched the leaves change colors on the trees like fire creeping down the mountainside. Her parents were not allowed to visit. The sanatorium was a treatment center, but also a place to segregate carriers of the disease. Some children did not see their parents for years. I can only imagine the cool mornings while mist rose from the river, the almost warm afternoons with the wind stirring the pines and clouds racing overhead. The season slowly changed to winter. Leaves scuttled along the ground in the wind. The skies turned from blue to gray. Still no one came. The dark arrived early. With the cold weather her cough grew fierce. She spent hours bent over the washbasin dredging up blood from her lungs, while white spots swam behind her eyes and the world outside the window blurred and distorted.

Every morning she was woken by the nurse's shoes going down the hall. During the day she sat in her room and watched the same rectangle of sky outside the wired windows. There were dozens, perhaps hundreds, of other children like her, with some plague growing inside them that kept them confined here, and I am sure they whispered to each other across the halls or put their heads close together as they sat outside in the warm afternoon, worried about what the future held for them. Perhaps they found something to laugh about as they called to one another down the vents that connected room to room, or wrote notes to one another in the margins of the books they read to pass the time. But mostly I imagine them watching the shadows of the sun move across the floor as the morning passed on, then watching the shadows the other way as night fell. They sat and tried not to stir the lungs as the moon and the stars came out and the sunlight on the floor through the window turned silver and the crickets grew so loud they could not hear. The girl wondered when her father would come for her, when she could go home. Her lungs grew worse. Her clothes grew red with spots of blood, small dots of darkness spraying from her when she coughed. When she breathed she could hear her lungs like dry bones clacking against one another.

One afternoon the nurses came down the hallway shutting the doors. The girl sat up in her bed, hoping they were coming for her. The doors closed one by one, reverberating like tombs, and when they stopped closing she lay on her stomach and peered beneath her door. In a few minutes a gurney with a squeaky wheel wobbled down the hall and stopped in front of one of the rooms. A doctor's black shoes went past. She heard a pen click, and muffled voices giving the date and time. When the gurney came back it did not squeak, weighted down with the body. She could not tell who it was, and would not find out until dinner came and they could look around to see who was not with them any longer.

As we toured the fourth and fifth floors, I kept thinking of her. I imagined one of my own daughters wandering the halls here. I imagined not being able to see her, imagined knowing she was locked away with disease clawing at her lungs.

And sometimes, since my return to North Carolina, I have imagined myself stuck in the Nyberg, walking each way down the long halls, past the empty rooms stacked one upon another, the doorways like eyes. I have imagined myself looking into each room, wondering where everyone has gone, much like how in memory, even now, I still wander through the house we lived in, still hear the voices floating on the summer air, ghosting through the buildings at night. There's a feeling an empty house has. Ours seemed to reverberate with space as we walked through that first time, our footsteps loud on the wood floors. I trailed a hand along the wall. My mother tried to be strong. The house was cold and empty and foreign. Alien, as if the ghosts of the last tenants still hovered there, and ours were somewhere in hiding, perhaps back in the house we had once lived in with my father. Now I wonder if the girl ever felt like that. Some days it seemed I did nothing but sit in my room. Sometimes it seems all we ever did was wait: for my father to come back; for us to move away from where we were; to start the next part of our lives.

I don't know how many times she heard the doors closing, although I do know the nurses closed the doors when someone died. Keeping spirits high was part of the treatment plan, and seeing bodies carted out would have reminded patients of what might happen to them.

I don't know how long she lived there, or why the belief in her ghost remains, although I suspect the ghost is a collective symbol, created out of the loss of what once walked the halls. There was not one girl but many, hundreds or thousands, and conjuring her ghost is a way to contain all the grief gathered in such a place.

Perhaps she lived there so long she forgot the house, the dusty road, her mother's face, her father's hands. Perhaps she could not recall them at all except for grainy pictures, like a memory of a dream. Perhaps she went through long periods of remission, and hope grew in her heart that one day she could breathe again, that she could rise from her bed and run down the long hallway and out into the sunlight and through the shadows of the pines trees, all the way down the hill and away. Or perhaps one day she realized she would never leave.

I don't know her name, or how long she has been roaming the halls.

I do know an estimated seventy thousand people came through the gates at the foot of the hill, though I do not know how many never left. The mortality rate of tuberculosis in the early 1900s was close to 30 percent. After the invention of antibiotics in the late 1940s, it fell to 10 percent, then even lower as antibiotics got better, as we learned more about treatment and prevention, but the outcome is too dreary to calculate.

Conventional paranormal wisdom tells us that ghosts are spirits trapped on this plane of existence, unable to find their way out. There were thousands of people who never found their way out of the Nyberg Building. Thousands who died there, who one day could not draw breath into their lungs and lay gasping and choking until the end. Are their spirits still in the Nyberg, entombed within the walls? And the ones who did make it out—do they ever return, either in body or memory or spirit? Do they find themselves waking from dreams of this place? Or am I the only other one, like the girl, wandering the halls and searching for something lost?

A few months after the last tuberculosis patients left the sanatorium, it became known locally as the Children's Colony because the first developmentally disabled residents to arrive were children. That was in 1973, a year after I was born. We moved there in 1980 and were sometimes woken by those strange calls in the night. There were rumors of ghosts even back then but we dismissed them because the real ghosts of our lives were enough to deal with.

The people who were confined there in my time carried out a sentence imposed by random genes, some imperfection in the DNA, whatever forces caused them to be the way they were. The tuberculosis patients must have felt the same thing, wondering why the wheel had spun in such a way.

Back in the conditioned air of the first floor, I shook my guide's hand. He told me to come back and he would take me through the old dormitories, the ancient chapel, the boiler room. I told him I would, and I meant it. What I didn't tell him was that I have never quite left. That might be too akin to saying I believe in ghosts, in things I can't see or hear or touch. But I want to believe that the girl on the third floor is as real as the stained sandstone of the crumbling buildings and the distant memories I have of living there, staring out the window and wondering where we were and how we had come to be there. If the girl is real, then we share the same past in the same place, with a similar hope for leaving it, and I can indulge the notion that we are all trapped by place and circumstance and random forces beyond our control, forever looking back with the sad silly sense that if we could just understand the tragic world we survived as children we could somehow be better adults, and our lives would fall into the neat categories we have created for them. It's not a perfect idea, but one I believed in driving down the hill as the Nyberg Building loomed softly in the rearview mirror.

WHERE WE
ARE GOING

All summer, my Sunday school teacher obsessed over sin and salvation. She skipped the stories of Daniel and the Lion's Den and Samson and Delilah, and went straight for the hard stuff: the Plains of Megiddo and the harrowing of Hell. She must have been about the age I am now, somewhere in the middle, when the realization that half our lives are over sets in. As she read, her voice sounded less of the school of love than the brink of fear, and when some parents complained that maybe eight was a bit too early to teach children about fire and brimstone, she said it was never too early, or too late, to prepare ourselves for the inevitable end.

When the summer ended she switched her sermons to service and sacrifice, which was the only way to keep out the sin and suffering, she said. We learned of the loaves and fishes, of Jesus in the garden of Gethsemane, right before the end. We heard His words on the cross, and she pushed her glasses back up her nose as she read in the close room, already older than Jesus ever was. On those days the story of Christ on the cross was not a warning but a welcoming, and it occurred to me years later that my Sunday school teacher saw the first as a way to reach the second. She told us of man's downfall in the Garden of Eden, then of Christ's sacrifice that absolved us all, but as a child the stories of sin stuck to me—I feared suffering in the lake of fire.

I did not know then that I would always be wondering which is stronger. Is it enough to not do the bad things, or does one have to do some of the good? Can we walk through the world in our own way or do we need to reach out for others? How does a man get inside the gate: by being absolved of all sins or by sacrificing himself? The Book of Job says it is not our lot to ask, but we've been asking since we came out of the cave, even when told blind obedience is the only way. Lot's wife looks back, questioning, and is turned to salt, which is a story I'm glad I never heard as a child because as a writer I am always looking back, trying to make some sense of the world.

This summer, when I visited my grandmother in the nursing home, where the suffering seemed to be all around, I was reminded of sin and salvation. Of warnings and welcomes, because this was where the old came to die. We call it caring for them, but we know they are close now, waiting, the same as all of us are, all our lives: we wait and we wonder. We look at the stars spinning above us, and we whisper words into the darkness to stave off what fears we hold inside.

Before I reached my grandmother's room, I saw my old Sunday school teacher in the hallway. Her body was bloated, skin strafed with liver spots; I was only sweating from the summer heat. She sat slumped in her wheelchair, staring at her hands. Slowly, she looked up at me. Her eyes had come unfocused. She didn't know me anymore, and my mother told me that she didn't know anyone, not family or friends or men who were once boys scared of what lay ahead of them. Let me say now we never prepare ourselves, not at eight or eighty, a thing I knew when she reached for my hand and asked the same old question: "Where am I?" she said. "Do you know where I am going?"

CHOKE

Chris and I fought in his front yard on a cold day in February. He was asleep when I got there and came out still groggy, hair messed up. He said, "Do we have to do this?" and I said, "It'll be over soon," or something just as stupid.

He came at me throwing hard straight punches. When his fist clipped my chin I saw stars, and after the second one caught me I covered up.

When he kept coming I dropped down and swept his legs. He was taller and quicker but I was stronger, so I took him to the ground and got on top. He turned his back and I wedged my elbow under his chin. I choked him until his arms weren't moving anymore.

In court the bailiff asked if I swore to tell the truth, the whole truth, and nothing but the truth. This essay only meets one of those requirements.

When I was in jail, the man in the cell next to me was trying to catch angels. He said they were hovering all around us. I could smell the whisky on him as he swiped at angels I couldn't see. He said they would protect him if he could catch one. He had only a few teeth. His face looked sunburned from years of cigarettes. I thought about telling him they wouldn't help him if he held them hostage, then realized he was telling himself a story that would let him continue living with something like hope.

Right now, if I have done what I am trying to do, you are thinking I went to prison for killing Chris.

Truth, but not the whole truth: I don't remember what month it was. I said February for the alliteration.

In Denis Johnson's book *Jesus' Son*, the narrator, Fuckhead, says, "Or maybe that wasn't the time it snowed. Maybe it was the time we slept in the truck and I rolled over on the bunnies and flattened them." As readers we are supposed to understand that Fuckhead can't tell the difference between what happened and what didn't happen. He doesn't know linear progression—the stories are all out of chronological order. His drug-addled mind gets mixed up, but I teach students that this is a trick by the writer. The writer remembers. And he arranged the stories in the order he wanted.

Let's try this again, a little more of the truth this time:
    Chris and I fought in his front yard on a day in a month I don't remember. He was taller and quicker than I was. He was also much younger. I was 27 at the time. He was 16. I held him down and choked him until his arms stopped moving.
    Tell me, how has the story changed? How much more of a monster am I now?

Irony: Tim O'Brien's "How to Tell a True War Story" is predicated on a lie. As are all stories, and the way we tell them.

"But how much can you make up in an essay?" a student asks.

"Nothing," I say. "But you can leave parts out."

In court that would be a lie of omission. In an essay it's called craft.

"Imagine," I say to my students, "telling your parents about the time you got in trouble at school. A fight or failing a class. Do you tell them everything unmitigated, or do you shade facts in your favor?"

I see the smiles of understanding, but I go on. "You were sent to the principal's office. On the way home are you working the story over in your head? Are you trying to make yourself sound sympathetic? Do you offer explanations? Do you tell your side—and only your side—of the story? Do you know your parents well enough to know what words will make them angry not at you, but at the other student/teacher/principal? Or to make them sorry for the punishment you've already received and so go softer on you?

"Isn't that the reason we tell stories? To move someone in the direction we want them to go?"

How, then, does the story change when I add more details? Chris was a skinny kid. He had a faint wisp of his first mustache. He was tall and quick but he was a kid and I was a grown man and I held him down and choked him until his arms stopped moving.

It was late May. The weather was already warm. I was sweating and breathing hard as I held him. His house—white, with blue trim—stood behind us. A silver Corvette—his

father's—was parked in the driveway. This was a neighborhood where women walked around the block every evening
after supper. A church stood on the corner.

In less than a year I would leave for graduate school to
learn to tell stories. Soon, Chris would be dead.

I'm still not telling the whole truth, because it's a hard truth to
tell. As are all the stories that sting. I'll argue the whole truth
can never be told anyway. There's too much of it.

I'm not sure what "Nothing but the truth" means either. For
example: what's the difference between "hold" and "choke"?
Between "kid" and "man"? Between "I left" and "he's dead"?

A warning: you will feel like I have lied. Let me assure you I
have not lied, except the lie of omission, although one might
argue that is the biggest lie of all, except in an essay, where
we call it craft. Call this crafted, then, if that helps.

In Flannery O'Connor's story "A Good Man Is Hard to Find,"
the grandmother should never have told The Misfit she rec-
ognized him. She should have kept it to herself, so she might
not have been killed.

But then that wouldn't have been the story O'Connor
wanted. It would not have been the truth she was looking for,
that, when finally faced with death, the grandmother lies.

Which brings us back to truth. And to stories, and how we
tell them. If I do not remember what Chris was wearing, I
have not told a lie. If I leave out the major parts of this story,
if I lead the reader to believe something that did not happen—a killing, perhaps—actually did happen, have I told a

lie? I would say yes, but the truth is that Chris is dead, and I saw a man trying to capture angels in a small jail cell in Western Arkansas not terribly long before I learned to tell stories.

The only lie is the choking part, and even that happened. Just not how I've said it did.

Let me add another piece: Chris's father watched us fight.

And another: Chris's father wanted us to fight.

And still another: Chris's father called Chris out of the house to fight.

What monster, you might be thinking, but let me assure you that is not the truth. When I called Chris's father after Chris's death we wept together on the phone.

An old professor of mine, when talking of details, used to say, "Don't tell me the couch is white unless someone will spill red wine on it later."

This is why I included the choking.

"The thousand injuries of Fortunato I had borne as I best could," Poe's narrator Montresor says in "The Cask of Amontillado," but gives no evidence of these injuries. He is an unreliable narrator, bending the story to his own being. The next line, "You, who so well know the nature of my soul," shows us the narrator is speaking to a priest, and since it's been fifty years since Montresor entombed Fortunato, we can assume it's his last confession. Montresor says in his rules for revenge that he must not get caught, and though he has not been caught in his earthly life, he fears the afterlife, so he is now confessing at death's bed to escape the hell in which he descended when he led Fortunato down to the catacombs.

But, again, unreliable. And the relish with which Montresor relates the story of the murder tells us that he will not be absolved by the priest. He might as well be swinging at angels.

Perhaps he should have left part of the story out. So I've revised it:

"Fortunato and I had a fight. Later, he died."

This is not meant to be suspense. I am just having a hard time getting where I need to go.

Here's a lie: In "A Rose for Emily," Emily Grierson tells the druggist she wants poison and the druggist writes "For Rats" on the arsenic he gives her.

Here's another part of the whole truth: I should have done something to save Chris.

So help me God.

One way of reading Poe's "The Tell-Tale Heart" is that there was no old man. The narrator is schizophrenic, and is trying to kill not the old man's eye, but the I of himself.

I am not trying to kill myself, only a memory of myself choking a young kid.

Part of that is a lie by omission. I did not choke Chris to death. I just wasn't there to help him find his breath.

One thing to remember in *Macbeth*: the witches did not lie. They just didn't tell the whole truth, which makes me wonder in how many of our literary stories the narrator lies to himself.

Once more unto the breach:

74 degrees and sunny. A day in late May, or early March. What the hell does it matter? Those aren't the important details. Don't get caught up in the unimportant details, the white couch. Wait for the red wine.

I was a student in Chris's father's martial arts class. Chris had already earned his black belt, and I was trying to earn mine. I had finished all my training and the only thing left was to see if I could defend myself, so Chris's father—whom I still call occasionally—got Chris out of the house and we fought in the front yard. He hit me twice and I took him to the ground, where I choked him until his arms stopped moving and he patted my leg. That's the part I've left out—he patted my leg. To tell me to stop. That he had given up.

Or maybe as you might pat someone on the back, like they have done something noble.

When I was sixteen or seventeen—around Chris's age on the day we fought—I began circling my small town in much the same way I circle stories now. Only then I had a bottle or a case of beer with me as I drove around and around. I was wondering what it meant to live in a place like this. Or to be alive at all, the great sky river rushing overhead and the summer breeze coming in the open windows, how still we get so sad at times we can't breathe. It seems I circled forever, until one night the blue lights came on behind me and I discovered something.

Then, I discovered the police put you in a jail cell for circling around and around after too much to drink.

Now, I know you put yourself inside a cell over the things you can't undo.

When the cop came to let the angel-catcher out, I stood against the bars.

"When do I get out?" I said.

"You still have a long ways to go," he told me.

"How do you plead?"
    "Guilty," I said.
    I still do.

"Write down the reasons you are telling this story," I say to my students, "and see what's at stake."

After the fight I helped him up. We hugged hard enough to hurt. At my black belt ceremony he sat beside me, beaming. It was the last time I ever saw him.

Because he was a kid. Because he looked up to me. Because I moved away. Because I never called to check on him. Because we lost touch. Because I was busy.

    Because I had forgotten how hard it is to be young. How often we turn to drink or drugs. I circled my small town for years wondering when I would leave it or finally feel alive. I don't know what happened to Chris. If he was trying to leave, or fighting to feel alive.

    Because I didn't ask.

He was studying to be a mental health therapist. I only found this out afterward, reading through the obituary late at night in a small circle of light from my lamp.

The angel catcher was still drunk when they led him out of the cell. He told the cop angels were watching over us all, and the cop said they better keep a closer watch on him.

A friend found Chris on the floor of his apartment. He had choked to death after the drugs got too far into his system for him to wake up.

I raised my hand. I told mostly the truth, but might have left out a few details.

"How do you know if it's ok to lie in nonfiction? Like, if no one will ever know?"

"You have to find the line you're not comfortable crossing."

Because I'm not comfortable with any of this. Because the guilt we take on when we lose someone can consume us. Because I feel guilty. I wanted you to think I killed Chris, because some days it feels that way.

"Getting choked sucks," Chris said afterward, and I said I only did it because he kept hitting me. That it hurt. I didn't tell him how we will do anything to stop our pain.

The omitted parts are, of course, the things that happened between then and now. Fill those in yourself. Just imagine phones not ringing, emails not answered. Imagine thinking, "I should call him back," and then never doing it.

I also tell my students the personal essay is always about the person, no matter the subject, which means this is about me. It's about stories, and how we tell them. But it's also about memory, and what we might have done.

How we should have checked on him sooner.

How we should have visited more often.

How we should have told him how much we loved him.

These are the things we say after it is too late. When we tear ourselves apart with all the things we might have done.

Because I want to remember standing in the front yard. We were both smiling. We shook hands. We bowed to one another. He was still smiling when he came at me and still smiling when his first straight right clipped my jaw. Still smiling when the second landed as well. He was still smiling when I swept his legs and still smiling when I put my arm around his neck. When he patted my leg. When he told me to stop. All of which makes me wonder what he was thinking when his life slipped away, if he wondered why no one was there to help him up.

A few questions, now that we're at the end: should I have held him down longer? Should I have never let him up? Would my friend still be alive if I could tell this story differently?

Because I left. Because I learned to tell stories. Because this is the story Chris can't tell. Because I promised to tell the whole truth.

THE BEAR

The woman, my grandmother said, lived all alone by herself way out in the woods. And some nights, while she was stirring her soap in a cauldron out back behind her house, stirring until her arms grew tired and her shoulders ached, she sang to herself a song of loneliness.

"Won't somebody come stay with me, stay with me, stay with me. Won't somebody come stay with me, all through the night."

And from far away, whispering through the woods in a low voice not unlike the woods themselves with their dark trees and darker shadows, came a voice saying, "I will."

And the woman stirred her soap then without singing, because the voice that rolled up out of the woods was full of fright, the voice of a murderer lurking in the darkness. She was scared, looking into the shadows where the wall of trees stood sentry to who knew what went on within. She'd heard stories, the woman had, and seen things, and some nights she feared the woods and what might come from them, more so when strange voices called back in answer to her song.

But soon she became lonely again, as she stirred her soap, even though her arms were tired and her shoulders sore, and she began to sing once again a song called up from her loneliness about wanting someone to come stay with her, stay with her, stay with her. Won't somebody come stay with her, all through the night.

And from the depths of the forest, though closer now, came the same low menacing voice saying, "I will," called out of the night as if some secret darkness were held within. The woman stopped her song and her stirring to stare into the trees at what was coming nearer. There was all manner of darkness in the world in those days, my grandmother said, late at night, my brother and cousins and I glancing out the window, where not far away the wall of trees began and the woods closed in. We could hear coyotes calling to one another and perhaps a few last wolves yet harboring in the blue hills, and there was indeed a wildness in the manner of the world when we were children. A sad note had crept into my grandmother's voice, much as the old woman stirring her soap, something of longing and loneliness, of waiting for what might come.

There were lines on her face, and sweat from the heat of the fire beneath the cauldron, a graying strand of hair that fell across her brow. And soon the loneliness overcame her once more, stronger than her fear of what might walk out of the woods. She began to sing once again.

"Won't somebody come stay with me, stay with me, stay with me. Won't somebody come stay with me, all through the night."

And right up close to the trees, which were right up close to the house, so close some nights she could hear the scratching of fingers as branches scraped the side, came the voice. "I will," the voice said, sung it, as if it were eager to come out of the woods. The woman stopped her stirring. She pushed back the graying strand with her shoulder. She turned toward the trees to see what waited therein. She did not like the woods nor living this close to them. Some mornings she hacked at the wall of trees and burned the old branches, but the trees in that forest in that part of the world in that time long ago grew dark and strong and repaired themselves at night, when the moon hung like a fingernail over the house.

"I will," the voice said, and in it came the echo of her longing. She looked hard at the wall of trees right up near the house where she stirred her soap. But soon again her loneliness was overcome by her fear and she began to sing once again. And as she sang and as she stirred and as she shouldered the graying strand from her lined face, a bear eased itself out of the woods and crossed the small short distance from the trees, dark and black and hoary as the first days of the world in its getting. The bear took the woman, and bore her off into the forest to eat her, and left behind there was only the soap, swirling, until it stopped and was still.

My grandmother told this story late at night when we stayed over and black storms were boiling up out of the west. "Won't somebody come stay with me," the woman sang, "all through the night." And from far away the bear sang back to her, his voice like a shadow on a tombstone, her voice like a gate swinging open. All stories are metaphor for what fears we hold inside, although I never understood this until many years later, when I learned my grandmother had been raped by a family friend when she was 14. She kept quiet for fear of what might be done to her if she told, and because of the shame others knowing would cause her. To leave the memory behind she hitchhiked across the state of Arkansas, trying to find family who would take her in, and while she was walking she was picked up by a man who bore a Bible on the seat beside him, but still tried to raise her dress to get at what was underneath. She got out of his car and walked until another car picked her up, this one steered by another man with the same impure thoughts, and in this way she made her way across the state, dodging danger in each car driven by men with something else on their minds.

I knew none of this late at night with the lightning flickering outside, drawing the world into shape. Not of her struggle, nor her stoicism in the face of it. She wore out her shoes while walking, and she wore out her voice telling men to leave her alone, just as she would sometimes wear out her voice telling stories to us late at night while the dark hung outside the window. She had lost her first child. She had lost a second one not long after that. Her first house had a dirt floor. Her second had no windows nor running water and when storms came she lay awake listening to the nails pulling away from the wood and wondering if her house would hold together. Like many women of her time she had no choice but to marry, and though she would eventually be carried off by a good man and forget how many others had tried to rape her, she still told the story, which makes me wonder now about the bear, and the woods, if she were trying to tell us something, or only repeating what she had heard once, as a child, when the world was a darker place.

PALM SUNDAY

Blessed is the King who comes in the name of the Lord, the congregation said, and we filed in waving our fronds. My grandfather sat in the third row, thin skin strafed with liver spots I thought were biblical, blood of Christ-like, his hair as thin as his skin. I was between eight and ten then and he was narrowing in on seventy, neither of us with any understanding of heaven or earth or what happens at the end of our days, despite what words were said during the sermons about sacrifice and salvation. This day, Palm Sunday, I had been waiting in the alcove, listening to the call and response of the catechisms, the organ reverberating through the walls, a sound I'm sure I remember thinking was angels, or spirits, something that hovered just beyond sight.

Even under the suspended lights—*light in heaven, light in our lives*—the church was dark. A narrow Jesus hung above the altar, pierced in five points. The carpet was blood red, thick beneath our small shoes. We knew then that Jesus rode into Jerusalem as the people laid down cloaks and small branches to pave his way into the city, but I'm not sure we knew reenacting his ride with our palm fronds was a way of easing our own souls into the skies. We listened to the low rumble of prayer, the deep-throated voices of old men reading and women mouthing the words, and maybe we thought of our own journeys, but I'm certain at that age we only whacked each other with our palm fronds, not yet worried whether our lives were everlasting.

I don't remember what we did when we reached the front, either. Whether we knelt and prayed, or placed our fronds on the floor beneath the feet of the crucified Christ. I've looked up the liturgy, words I've lost through the distance of memory, but I'll leave them alone, except to say that the words we said were for eternal life and the blessing of our fathers. For safe passage into Jerusalem, which is beyond this world.

Who knew then about eternity, or how hard we'd be hit by loss years later? I only remember seeing my grandfather as I went past with my palm frond, his skin so thin by then it split under any scratch, any borne bruise. He was smiling at me, proud in that moment, and I remember thinking of this the morning after he died. When the phone rang late the night before I didn't hear it, lost in whatever call and response I re-enact at my computer, trying to breathe words back to life. His heart, my brother told me, had been gripped by a fierce heat, which made me think of how Jesus' last words were either of being forsaken or of finality, as if not even a god knows how to go into the afterlife.

I've since come to think that the words we recite rarely matter. There will always be room for wishes, ways we will hurt ourselves over the moments we've missed. In the awful morning still standing in my thin skin, I thought that instead of writing or recreating the world—whatever it was that kept me from the phone—that I should have been speeding through the skies toward Arkansas. Imagine if I had arrived in time: my family all gathered by the bed, laying down branches to soothe his last breaths, hoping to ease his passage through the gates with all the things they never said.

A BRIEF AND SELECTED HISTORY OF MAN, DEFINED BY A FEW OF THE WALLS HE HAS BUILT

THE ALPHA AND OMEGA

Our lives begin and end with walls. From the uterine walls we enter this world through, to our final resting place, we are surrounded. Formed from seminal fluid surging through canals, we are then suspended in serous liquid, awash in amniotic sacs. From bodies, we become body, embraced in the warmth of the womb. Once born, we are wrapped in blankets or enclosed in incubators while grandparents and friends stand peering through more walls made of glass. Encased in car seats on the ride home we are then carried to our cradles, always cuddled, our mother's warm hands cupping our tiny heads.

From cradles we move to cribs, slightly larger, the walls formed of bars from where we watch the outside world. Mobiles spin above us like stars but we are still enclosed, until we graduate from cribs to beds and are then tucked in tightly at night and offered wards formed from words to keep us safe: *sleep tight, don't let the bedbugs bite,* which I know has a historical meaning but I tend to think of, metaphorically, as our attempt to prevent outside forces from passing between our carefully constructed walls and somehow harming us.

Once free from the crib we still stay indoors. Around the walls of my daughters' bedroom stand dressers and shelves of books like a second wall inside the first. On rainy afternoons we sit inside reading while the rain runs in rivulets down the windows or the first frost forms on the glass, adding another layer. As we grow older we leave our houses and board buses to school, or climb in cars to drive to our offices. We walk through narrow corridors to enter classrooms or cubicles, more walls within walls, where we spend most of our days before driving back home, the world moving outside the glass, and when we grow old we move out of our large houses into smaller apartments as the space becomes too much, and we wish to return to something simpler.

Tombs are the last walls we inhabit, when outside forces erode our mortal shells. In New Orleans, tombs have become part of the beauty of the city. The ground is saturated with water, so bodies buried below ground rise to the top as if they are floating back into the world. The tombs are elaborate, carved with angels and crosses. They house entire families. After hundreds of years the wooden caskets rot, and the bones intermingle inside.

Our oldest archaeological finds are tombs. In 209 or 210 BC the emperor Qin Shi Huang of China was buried in an underground tomb with over 8,000 warriors carved from earth. The terracotta warriors are life-sized. No two are alike. They vary in dress, hairstyle, and height, depending on rank. According to the historian Sima Qian, the terra cotta warriors were to help the emperor rule another empire in the afterlife. The mausoleum, Sima Qian wrote, held one hundred rivers of mercury, palaces, treasures, and towers, and above this the heavenly bodies, all enclosed within the earth.

The largest and most lavish tombs in the world are the Great Pyramids. For 3,800 years the Great Pyramid of Giza was the tallest building in the world. It is comprised of 2.3 million stones, some of them dragged, floated, or rolled from

500 miles away. The pharaoh Khufu, for whom it was built, was seen as a god, and the tomb a continuation of his divinity. It was not simply a tomb, but a causeway between heaven and Earth only he could use.

The smallest tombs in the world are caskets designed for miscarriages in the first trimester. They measure 10 inches by 5 inches by 4 inches. They are lined with flannel for warmth and are glued forever closed. They are small enough to hold in your hands.

WITH WORDS COME WALLS

By the time man learned to form words into history he had also learned to form the earth into fortifications. In much the same way clay tablets were shaped to accept cuneiform or ancient plants pressed to hold hieroglyphics, our ancestors erected walls. They were formed of dirt held together with water and dried or burned into bricks, or stone dug from the earth and dragged in place and chiseled by peoples so distant from us today we have few records of them other than the earth they left behind.

The Hittites, Sumerians, Egyptians, Babylonians, Akkadians, Trojans, and Assyrians all built walls around their cities. They expanded and developed and traded the knowledge of erecting fortifications by attacking one another, learning through trial and error the strengths and weaknesses of opposing walls. When he felt Babylon vulnerable to attack, Nebuchadnezzar reinforced the city with a wall and moat inside the old walls, forming a double line of fortifications. In the palaces of Assyria towers guarded gates, and wall-walks and embattled parapets sat atop the walls. In the vast distances of history, even small cities stood protected by walls.

The remains of some of these walls and ancient forts still stand, although our knowledge of their completed form comes not from the crumbling ruins but from art. On the south wall of the Great Hypostyle Hall of the Ramesseum, one drawing shows the besieged city of Dapour of the Hittites. Atop the crenellated walkways and towers, the Hittites attempted to hold back the attacking Egyptians with spears and arrows and rocks. The Egyptians advanced using long shields while the Hittites rained down arrows from the three walls. From the keep in the center of the city wooden boards were extended, and the Hittite soldiers fought from these boards as well. The Egyptians, upon reaching the walls under the cover of their shields, raised scaling ladders. A few of them made it to the top, and were thrown to the ground.

SO MANY FORTS, SO CLOSE TO HOME

I grew up a few miles away from Fort Chaffee, one of the largest live-fire forts in the US. On weekends National Guard and Air Guard units dropped bombs on the surrounding hills, and the windows in our houses rattled and shook. When we drove through Fort Chaffee, MPs stared at us with mirrored eyes. F-16s flew overhead, and artillery fired in the distance. Some days the roads were closed to civilians, and other days fresh patches of asphalt marked where bombs had strayed off target.

Fort Chaffee butted up against Fort Smith, which in the early 1800s had been a frontier military post, but was now a city of 75,000 people. A few hours east were Camp Robinson and Jackson Air Force Base and Pine Bluff Arsenal, one of six Army installations in the US that store chemical weapons. In the early 1960s my grandfather applied for a job at Pine Bluff Arsenal. After interviewing inside the facility that made chemical weapons out of unhatched chicken eggs, he did not accept the position.

In 1990, when Saddam Hussein invaded Kuwait, I was in Fort Sill, Oklahoma, another large, hot, live-fire fort where the earth randomly shook around us from the force of bombs. A year later I went to Fort Jackson in South Carolina, where it rained every afternoon at four, and then the ground steamed in the humidity after the rain. During one weekend of my National Guard service, my unit flew to Fort Hood, Texas, for training. Our C-130 landed on a remote airstrip at noon, and because the fort was so large night was falling before the buses arrived to pick us up. I remember the miles and miles of scrub brush and mesquite, faint breaths of wind in the hot afternoon, shadows stealing slowly across the landscape, making it almost pleasant to be where we were.

In the mid-'90s, not long after I left the military, I worked for a time in Missouri. Driving through the countryside one afternoon I found myself on Fort Leonard Wood. I was lost and asked an MP for directions. He was polite, but his mirrored sunglasses unnerved me. I was sure that I would somehow be forced to rejoin.

A year after that I was in Colorado Springs, Colorado, where the Air Force Academy shimmers in the shade of the mountains that NORAD hides under. Now I live in North Carolina, only an hour's drive from Fort Bragg, home of the US Special Forces. To the west lies Fort Fisher, a confederate fort during the Civil War. To the north is where Camp Butner used to be. During World War II it served as a deployment area for the western front. Now the camp has been incorporated as the township of Butner, which is home to several state and federal prisons.

There are roughly 450 military bases in the United States. Worldwide, there are between 700 and 900 United States military bases in over 150 countries. New bases have been built in seven countries since September 11, 2001. There are thirty-eight large and medium-sized American facilities around the world, mostly air and naval bases for our bombers and fleets. In 1898, at the height of imperialism, Great Britain controlled thirty-six naval bases and army garrisons. In 117 AD the Roman Empire required thirty-seven major bases to police its realm from Britannia to Egypt, from Hispania to Armenia.[1]

---

1. Johnson, Chalmers A. *Nemesis: The Last Days of the American Republic.* Metropolitan Books, 2007.

A few years ago, over one hundred acres of Fort Chaffee caught fire. The old barracks burned, and afterward with smoke rising from the ash of the buildings like ghosts, the land looked like war had come, or that the bombs that had always fallen finally missed their mark.

From my computer desk I can look out my window into the backyard and see two different walls. One is my fence separating my yard from my neighbor's. The other is his fence separating his yard from mine. I am not counting the window, or the wall that encases it.

WALLS IN THE WORD

In the Bible, the difference between a city and a town was defined by walls. Much of the Old Testament deals with physical walls; much of the New Testament deals with metaphorical walls. The Old Testament depicts stories of fallen cities and gives rules on how to lay siege to one; the New Testament says that a man without faith is like a city without a wall.

When the Israelites crossed the Red Sea, the water stood like a wall to either side of them. In their search for the promised land they encountered many walled cities, and utterly destroyed them all. When they reached the city of Jericho they circled the city for six days. On the seventh day they sounded their trumpets and the walls fell.

When Nebuchadnezzar marched against Jerusalem he laid siege against it for a year and a half, until famine ensued within the city and the walls were breached.

The walls of Sodom and Gomorrah were said to be destroyed by fire and brimstone. The walls of Nineveh were said to be destroyed because of pride.

The book of Deuteronomy tells what would happen to a city should the inhabitants become corrupt, warning that God would bring a nation against them as swift as the eagle flies, and that nation shall besiege them in all their towns, until the city's high and fortified walls, in which they trusted, came down throughout the land.

In these cases, one supposes, walls were of little use.

Many of the ancient cities of the Bible have been destroyed, their walls swept clean, stone returned to stone. But some still exist, those that were not proclaimed from on high to be destroyed, ancient stone or mud-baked brick surviving through the centuries in crumbled capacity. In Jerusalem's old city a 3,700-year-old wall was recently discovered. And it is in Jerusalem, atop the Temple Mount, that three religions worship, side by side by side, which is heartening, if we can forget the number of times the city has been besieged by one religion or the other.

THE FALL OF ROME AND
THE AGE OF CASTLES

In Europe, the Middle Ages began and ended with falling walls. In 476 CE Augustus Romulus was forced to abdicate the Roman throne, and the Western Roman Empire ceased to be. With the fall of Rome, safe travel, a dependable agricultural system, and administrative and military infrastructure disappeared. The walls of Rome were destroyed by the invaders. They would later be rebuilt and torn down again as Rome changed hands over hundreds of years.

A thousand years later Constantinople fell to the Ottoman Empire, and many Byzantine scholars fled to the west, bringing with them important Greek texts and a revival of learning. The Hundred Year's War ended, the Moors were expelled from the Iberian Peninsula, and Columbus found the New World, ushering in the Age of Discovery and destroying the walls of ignorance and isolation that had surrounded Western civilization since Rome fell. The printing press was invented, destroying even more.

Ironic then, that for the thousand years of the Middle Ages, society was formed by walls. The first half of the Middle Ages, from roughly the fifth to the tenth centuries, were marked by "barbarian" invasions as Vandals and Visigoths and various Scandinavian and Eastern European tribes poured into Central and Western Europe. In territories that had been part of the Roman Empire, stone fortified cities stood against the waves from the north. Beyond the old Roman Empire, wooden walls, or structures made of earth and wood, defended cities and villages. Without walls, there was nowhere to run when the barbarians howled at the gates.

From the tenth to the fifteenth century and the end of the Middle Ages, the castle dominated the landscape. Everywhere there were walls: Roman fortifications, wooden towers and stone observations posts, cities walled by palisades. Monasteries and cathedrals were fortified with walls, turrets, crenellated battlements, and murder holes. Local lords built castles with moats and drawbridges. The invading barbarians had settled the lands, and a rise in agriculture brought with it a stability of social order in the way of the feudal system, though the peasants were often trapped by the very walls that protected them, both the real walls of the villages or castles, and the walls of caste society. The nobility wore plate armor and heavy shields and rode on armored horses, which makes me think of an era when some could afford their own protective walls to carry around with them.

The walls of the Middle Ages did not last. The Mongols swept through Eastern Europe, destroying cities. The cannon was invented. At the Battle of Agincourt, protected only by terrain and sharpened stakes slanted into the ground, English longbowmen cut down the heavily armored French. The cannon effectively brought down the high walls of the castle. The longbow, and the arrival of the rifle, changed the nature of armor, and war. The Crusades ignited a desire to travel, the Renaissance a reconnection with Roman and Greek learning. What castles still stand are admired as architecture, or archaeology.

My office is on the third floor of an ivy-encrusted brick building. Around me stand other brick buildings, arranged like a fort, and many days I sit and stare out the window at the people moving below. Counting the ivy and the brick and the insulation, I am thickly encased, protected from siege.

WALLS IN WAR

What walls we conquer or conjure, what forts we form to protect us, all fail and wither, whether to time or tide of the slow erosion from forces beyond our ability to keep out.

In the 1460s, after years of war against the Ottoman Empire, Vlad the Impaler, from whom our modern stories of Dracula are derived, found himself besieged inside his own castle by the Ottoman forces. Surrounded by an army and trapped within the walls her husband had built, his wife threw herself from the battlements into the river below so the Ottomans would not torture her. Vlad escaped with the help of villagers who turned their horseshoes backward and led him out in the dark of night.

In 1754 George Washington and his Virginia Militia marched on Fort Duquesne to capture it and drive the French from the region. When he realized that the fort was too heavily defended, he retreated and built Fort Necessity, deciding that if he could not rid the area of the French, he would at least establish his own presence nearby. When the French surrounded the fort in early July, Washington was greatly outnumbered. It was the only time Washington would ever surrender, and was the first action in the French and Indian War.

In December of 1835, Texas volunteers marched on and captured the Alamo near San Antonio De Bexar. Less than three months later General Antonio López de Santa Anna laid siege to the city. On the morning of March 6, 1836, Mexican troops stormed the walls. They captured a cannon atop the walls and turned it against the barricaded church where the defenders had holed up, and blasted open their last line of defense.

The first shots fired in the Civil War landed on the walls of Fort Sumter when it would not surrender to the newly formed Confederacy. The French Revolution began with the storming of the walls of the Bastille.

After World War I the French built the Maginot Line, a 1,300-mile long series of defenses, which the Germans simply bypassed when invading France in World War II. Paris fell a few weeks later, and France surrendered.

The demilitarized zone in Korea is a 160-mile-long, 2.5-mile-wide stretch of land that cuts the Korean peninsula in half. On either side, north and south, are guards and gates, fences topped with concertina wire stretching to distance in each direction. Inside it are tank walls and mine fields. It is the most heavily militarized border in the world.

In the early eighties President Ronald Reagan proposed his "Star Wars" plan, which was, in effect, a defensive wall in outer space.

Though Fort Leavenworth, Kansas, is home to two colleges, a mechanized infantry division, and a university, it is most famous for its walls designed to keep people in, not out.

Fort Knox, Kentucky, is designed to keep gold in and people out.

When my daughters were little my wife and I would wake some nights to check on one of them and find her standing in her crib holding onto the slats and peering out through the gaps. I do not know now if we were keeping them in so they did not hurt themselves or attempting to keep out what might hurt them.

SMALL SPACES

When I was a child, the old storm cellar behind our house was a perfect fort. It had a narrow entrance, guarded by stone walls. From the top you could survey approaching danger.

On hot summer nights with the door closed we could hear the storms howling outside, but inside we were protected from whatever was waiting on the other side. It was small and damp and smelled like earth. Lightning flashed through the cracks in the door and sometimes rainwater crept in, but we huddled together until it was safe to go back out.

Now, on rainy afternoons, I stretch sheets across my daughters' bedroom upstairs, stack couch cushions to create our own small enclosures. A heavy quilt hangs from the top bunk bed to the bottom, forming a fort inside. My daughters peer out from small spaces, smiling. The thunder reminds me of old bombs while my children crawl through tunnels we have made with whatever is on hand, connecting bunk bed fort to lean-to couch. My wife surveys the room, wondering how long it will take to tear down our fortress and re-arrange our walls into some semblance of order, and watching my daughters, I fear the day they will outgrow this sort of thing, when what walls surround them will not be of my making.

For thousands of years man has built walls to protect him. The walls we build now are for comfort, and since they do not need to protect us from marauding armies, they can be made of anything. As children we crawl into boxes, retreat into the cool shade beneath magnolia trees on hot afternoons, or where two cedars have grown close together and in winter snow hangs in the boughs overhead. We listen beneath bridges while cars hum overhead, or climb barn lofts to hide in the hay. We slip beneath the sink when no one is looking and close the cabinet doors behind us. We slide into the crawl space or the closet beneath the stairs, keep our secret code words and share them with only the most intimate of friends. In tree houses, in basements and cellars and attics, we enclose ourselves within walls, seek out small spaces to remind us from where we have all come.

As we grow older we search for basements or workshops or hobby rooms, offices or backyards or porches, some place to be alone for a little while. We surround ourselves with wilderness or technology, space or enclosure, whichever feels the most like a fort, and when we finally grow old we fold ourselves into boxes and inter ourselves to the earth. We spend our lives looking for walls to surround us, whether it's a couple of couch cushions stacked in a square or a six-foot sheet stretched between shelves or the perfect house from which we will build our memories. Whether it's a bed or a bottle or a narrow writing room or a memory from long ago. Some place we feel the sense of safety we only knew while in the womb.

The Bible describes heaven as a city of gold, with walls of jasper. There are twelve gates, three to the cardinal directions, each gate made of precious stones. The walls of the city have twelve foundations, and they are as high as the city is long, which makes me wonder what needs to be kept out.

THE GIVING OF FOOD

When my grandmother was little, she stole a chicken leg from the adults' table during Sunday dinner. This was in the '30s, sometime during the heart of the Great Depression. For some reason that escapes me the adults ate first, and my grandmother couldn't wait. While the adults were settling down—I always imagine them unfolding their napkins, bowing their heads to say Grace—my grandmother, six or seven at the time, lunged for the table. She swiped a chicken leg from a plate, dragged it through the gravy, and ran out the back door.

There is little else to the story. No condemnation or punishment, at least not in my grandmother's memory. She was so young she remembers nothing but the act itself—the quick dash across the kitchen, the surprised faces of her mother and father and aunts and uncles and, I like to imagine, the jealous faces of her brothers and sisters and cousins. Sometimes I imagine them chasing her from the table, stumbling as they push back their chairs, hurling threats behind her and scrambling after her as if she were a stray dog that had somehow wandered in. I see my grandmother flinging open the back screen door, scurrying down the short set of stairs, and sprinting across the backyard. She hides in a cluster of trees, or crouches down behind a shed somewhere, gravy running down her arm as they call to her.

I'm sure it is wrong, however. I'm sure no one chased her. More likely they watched her run out the door, then smiled to each other, laughing a bit, as they passed the mashed potatoes. When she finally came back in, after hours of hiding, her stomach rumbling after only one chicken leg, I'm sure they had a plate saved for her, kept warm in the oven, and her mother sat beside her as she ate, asking her if she wanted another hot roll or another helping of potatoes.

When I relive this story in my head, I see my grandmother not at six or seven, but the way she is now—thirty pounds overweight, her skin beginning to sag; skin that looks scalded, white spots on her fleshy arms; her hair formed in a perfect bowl from hours under a hair dryer at the beauty shop. Her eyes are slightly glazed with age. She smells faintly of powder and hair spray and church.

The kitchen is nothing, I'm sure, like the kitchen of her childhood, a small kitchen in a rented house somewhere on a dirt road where horse and buggy were still more common than automobiles. In that kitchen would have been a woodstove, unpainted walls or walls that had faded to the dusty color of the land outside. The hardwood floors would be thick with dirt, though my great-grandmother would have had the same hatred for uncleanliness as my grandmother. A few loose cabinets stood to either side of a rust-colored sink. I see an open door, and, though I know it is somewhat melodramatic, dust blowing across the fields outside the window. The men are in overalls, sweaty and hot from a hard day of work in the fields. The women—each balancing a young child or two at their side—wear plain dresses sewn by hand, and the children, many of them, cluster underfoot until the women chase the younger ones away and put the older ones to work.

This is a different time, and because I can see it only through stories, it does not seem real. The real image is my grandmother's kitchen, and she is not six or seven and sitting in a corner contemplating stealing a chicken leg but standing at the stove stirring gravy in slow circles. It is hot in the kitchen, the gas burners ticking quietly, steam rising from beneath closed lids. The stovetop and the kitchen counter are thick with dishes: baked ham and mashed potatoes with giblet gravy, corn and green beans and fried okra, hot rolls and homemade bread, sliced tomatoes and cucumbers and onions, deviled eggs, four or five pies.

My grandmother stands at the stove in her church clothes—she has woken at four or five that morning to cook before going to church with my grandfather—wondering aloud what she has forgotten. My mother moves in silently to help her, though most of the work has been done already. My grandmother and mother uncover the dishes. They set the plates out on the counter, shoving trays of deviled eggs and pans of fresh-baked bread aside to make room. In the other room the men sit waiting, and when my grandmother appears in the doorway telling everyone to come eat, we file in one by one to gather around the table. My grandmother lists each article of food in case anyone has recently forgotten what ham is, or corn, and it is at this moment that I imagine my grandmother at six or seven, streaking through the house dripping a trail of gravy that anyone could follow, like a path through the twists and folds of time that separate then and now.

Perhaps because she grew up in a time of next to nothing, my grandmother's meals are plentiful. They are not extravagant, and we do not dine on fine china, but there is never a shortage of food, as there often was during her childhood in the Great Depression. I think, perhaps, the men ate first because they needed the strength to work, or search for work, but in my mind I see the women not eating at all, or eating very little, so that the children would not go hungry.

My grandmother eats last, after everyone else has been fed. She hovers over the table as we eat, offering seconds on potatoes, another slice of ham, more hot rolls. She fills glasses with milk, or replaces dropped knives and forks. When she finally sits to eat, she eats well. I wonder if some vestige of fear still lurks in her memory from her childhood, when there was not enough food to go around. I can see it in the way she watches over us, making sure we have eaten enough. I'm sure there were times when she went hungry, when there was not enough money to buy food; I'm sure her father's greatest fear was not being able to feed his family, and after she has eaten, after she has fed her family, she seems happy, finally satisfied.

Often, over the years, I've seen her prepare a plate, or two or three plates, wrapping them in cellophane and driving them to shut-ins or the poor or simply people she believes might need a good meal. In the houses to either side of hers invariably lived widows, women even older than my grandmother whose children lived in different states and rarely visited. Sometimes she would invite them to Christmas dinner, or Thanksgiving, if she had word that their relatives would not be visiting this year, if she was afraid they would be alone, and hungry.

She took food to church functions, to friends and neighbors, and to funerals. When her younger brother died many years ago, and then my grandfather much later, her house was filled with people and the food they brought: green-bean casseroles and meat loafs, baked chicken and pecan pie, scalloped potatoes and homemade bread, sweet peas and corn relish. Eating seems to lessen the tragedy of death somehow, to remind us that we are alive, but I've always thought my grandmother grieved longer because with all the food others brought, she was not allowed to cook, to provide for all the people in her house who were there to comfort her.

Our language is stuffed with food.

Man cannot live on bread alone. You are what you eat. The quickest way to a man's heart is through his stomach.

An apple a day keeps the doctor away; the apple of my eye; Adam's apple. Honey catches more flies than vinegar.

When we get together to eat we break bread. To put food on the table means to provide for your family. To bring home the bacon means almost the same. When we do well we enjoy the fruits of our labor. Not my cup of tea means you don't particularly enjoy that item. When we want to say someone is strange or crazy we call them fruits, or say they are nuts. Bread and butter are the basic survival needs of a person; to butter someone up is to flatter them for personal gain. A piece of cake means something is easy; to sell like hotcakes means to sell well. Cars can be souped up; a person can have egg on his face. They can also be a bad egg or be cool as a cucumber. It is generally considered bad if one cries over spilt milk, or has a finger in every pie. Most people believe you cannot make an omelet without breaking a few eggs. One of my greatest fears as a child was jail, where, my uncles told me, you were fed bread and water, nothing else.

Every country has their proverbial sayings of food. In *Don Quixote*, Cervantes told us that "all sorrows are less with bread." Marie Antoinette supposedly said "let them eat cake" (missing the point entirely). In England, proverbs abound, from the morose "He that eats till he is sick must fast till he is well" to the glib "After dinner sit a while, and after supper walk a mile."

Thanksgiving is a celebration almost entirely of food, an amalgamation of European harvest festivals and thanks giving to Native Americans, without whom many early European settlers to the New World would not have survived. In typical American fashion it has now been dubbed the insidious Turkey Day, suggesting only a day where turkey is eaten, rather than a celebration of food, of life.

Stories of food illuminate some of our greatest Biblical lessons. When the prodigal son returns, his father kills the fatted calf to welcome him home. Job first learns of the attacks on his livestock while he is eating. The Old Testament holds numerous examples of feasts, beginning with the feast Abraham gave the angels in Genesis 18:1–8; kitchen supply lists of the court of Solomon in Kings 1, 2–3; and in Samuel 2, 17:28–9, where three chieftains honor David and his court in lavish fashion.

Jesus turned water into wine. For communion we take of the body and blood of Christ, a symbolic idea that faith is sustenance, sustenance faith, that one cannot be separated from the other. When we eat, we are alive. Jesus' last act with his disciples was to break bread, to eat of the body and blood.

But perhaps Jesus' greatest feat was when he fed a multitude with only a few fishes and loaves, his divine powers called on to provide for all. According to the story, five thousand men and women ate, and there were twelve baskets left over. I suppose it would be too much to ask that there be a chicken leg in there somewhere, but I like to think of the leftovers being passed out according to need, so that even those with nothing might have another meal.

My grandmother worked for thirty years in a cafeteria. She woke somewhere around three in the morning, and, because she did not like to drive at night, woke my grandfather to take her to work. She worked at a home for the developmentally disabled, arriving each morning at 3:30, the streetlights muted, the pines among the buildings of the institute dark, the buildings themselves silent.

Inside, the cafeteria smelled of steam and heat, the big ovens just firing up. Pots and pans clanged together. The floor was always wet, dark red tile set here and there with drains. Long stainless steel counters ran along the walls, broken only by the big ovens, eyes flickering blue flame beneath boiling pots, the long griddles sizzling. For hours my grandmother would prepare dough for biscuits, her sleeves rolled back, hands encased in plastic, her hair caught by a hairnet. Steam hung thick in the air, and her face would be red, tired before first light.

Between six and eight they served breakfast. The institute housed hundreds of residents, long lines shuffling past, trays held out in supplication. Here I imagine my grandmother spooning grits, or passing biscuits, smiling as the residents nod to her.

When breakfast was over they cleaned the entire kitchen, wiping down every surface, scrubbing each pot, each pan. The plastic trays went into a steam machine, steam roiling thickly, hovering in the kitchen, and after everything had been wiped down, sterilized, and wiped down again, they began cooking lunch, vast towers of potatoes waiting to be peeled and blanched, meat prepared, vegetables diced, and after lunch they did it all again, cleaning, sterilizing, starting over.

She would come home sometime before dinner, late in the afternoon. Tired and sore, she would sit quietly in the den for a time, staring down into the folds of her hands, occasionally nodding off. She was there when my brother and I walked to her house after school. When I was old enough to become aware of her job I was embarrassed that she was a cafeteria worker, thankful that she didn't work in the cafeteria at my elementary school. She would smile when we walked in, then struggle upward from her chair to cook us something to eat.

A typical visit to my grandmother's house:
  My grandmother: Are you hungry?
  Me: No, thank you. I'm fine.
  Her: Let me fix you something to eat.
  Me: I couldn't eat a bite.
  Her: There's some ham from yesterday.
  Me: I'm full as a tick.
  Her: Deviled eggs, I think. And corn. Mashed potatoes.
  I'm about to burst.
  Macaroni and cheese. Giblet gravy. Hot rolls.
  . . . (representing a silence in which words of denial have failed me)
  Fried chicken. Sliced onions. Cucumbers. Tomatoes.

. . . (and another)

I can fry you some eggs. With hash browns.

. . . (and another)

There's pecan pie. And cookies.

Maybe I'll have a small plate.

What she brings me would feed ten people. I am not allowed to help in any way, but must sit quietly while she rushes around the kitchen, humming slightly under her breath. When she puts the plate before me she sits and watches me eat. She looks hurt if I begin to push the plate away.

You want dessert, don't you?

I say maybe later I'll have a piece of pie. This seems to placate her, though she looks at me as if she is not sure whether she can trust me, as if I might slip away before she is satisfied that I have eaten enough, and might suddenly become famished.

Steinbeck immortalized people of my grandparent's generation, the time of dirt and red sun, farms disappearing under miles of dust or signs of foreclosure, worthless crops left to stand in the fields. The Joads went west, searching for promises. They found none but the will to live, and the basic humanity, in the end, to provide for others.

His novel is as much about food as anything else. Food drives the Joads west—both the constant hunger and the promise of work in the fields and orchards. He constantly reminds the reader of the gnawing pain of hunger, the fear of famine and the violence that fear may spawn, and though Steinbeck says little of the people who stayed put, their struggle was the same: the struggle to put food on the table, to bring home the bacon.

I have no connection to that time but the collective memory of a fading generation, old reels splotted with age of dust storms and abandoned towns, long lines of cars heading west or people standing alongside the road beside a car that has broken down, usually holding a hand-lettered sign that says "California or bust," and a grandmother who refuses to let her family go hungry, long after the possibility of it has disappeared.

I rarely saw her actually cook. More often in my mind the work has been done behind the scenes, as when she cooked early, before church, or when she would call to tell my mother that everything was ready and we had better hurry or it would be cold. Most times when we arrived the table would be set, the dishes on the stove uncovered, everything made ready. Or else, if we arrived a few minutes early so my mother could help her, my grandmother would be bustling about, making the last preparations, calling for everyone to come on and eat.

If she was not in the kitchen she would be in her chair, half-dozing, the ceiling fan wicking slowly above her. My grandfather whiled away his time in front of the television, but my grandmother rarely joined him, instead opting to sit quietly, staring out the open front door at the street or staring down at her hands. In the mornings she would be in her house robe, sipping coffee; in the afternoon, tired from work, she would drink a tiny glass of Coke.

Other postures common to her were watering the flowers on her front porch; raking leaves and pine needles in the backyard; working in the garden until arthritis and the summer heat forced her inside; coming slowly down the hall from her bedroom; holding one of my cousins or, later, daughters, for hours at a time, both of them near sleep, my grandmother cooing softly or singing nonsense songs in a soothing voice.

When I see her cooking in memory, it is always one of the meals that I liked best. Flour spread out on a cutting board, she is rolling dough for dumplings, then quickly cutting the dough into thin, flat pieces. In a dutch oven chicken boils until it falls off the bone, and, when it is ready, she will drop the dumplings into the boiling broth while she pulls the chicken from the bone. Or she is rolling steaks in flour, laying them carefully in hot grease. After the steaks have cooked she will make the gravy, a thick brown gravy that settles into the bones and forces you to either walk it off or settle onto the couch for most of the afternoon, the ceiling fan ticking away above you, the television humming faintly in the other room.

When she cooked, she worked quietly and quickly, no motion wasted. Her face would be set in a grim line, but I suspect it had little to do with her mood. Rather, here was a job, and only after it was done—after the family had been taken care of—could she enjoy the fruits of her labor.

Every few years she has the kitchen repainted. It is now bright pink, a color that should be ugly in a kitchen but is not. Hung above the cabinets, just below the ceiling, are commemorative plates of the fifty states. I do not know where or when she got them; they have been there always.

Above the table, on the wall opposite a window that looks out on the backyard, is a painting of a vase filled with flowers. The vase throws a delicate shadow. One of the flowers is drooping. It is an inexpensive painting, oil on canvas, probably picked up at a yard sale thirty or forty years ago.

There are actually two tables. The big table sits in what is euphemistically called a dining room, an eight by ten section of floor separated from the kitchen only by a waist high counter. It is covered with a tablecloth at all times. A vase of flowers, similar to the picture that hangs above, sits in the center of the table, though at Thanksgiving, the flowers are replaced by a paper turkey.

The other table is in the kitchen, just a few feet away from the stove. It is here, by some unspoken harkening back to the past, that the children sit. Or when I have visited at some odd hour—I once worked third shift and would stop by for breakfast after getting off work—that I am fed, my grandmother sitting beside me, watching me eat. She sips her coffee loudly. She is not wearing her false teeth, the shape of her mouth strange as she talks, her words slurred slightly as if she has suffered a stroke. Without makeup, her face is almost white, etched deeply with wrinkles.

It is hard to see her as a child. She was the oldest of eight, and it seems she was born taking care of people: first her younger siblings, then her own children, followed by an aging mother who could not walk, then grandchildren, great-grand-children. A meal for her might have consisted of dough fried in lard and a scrap of salt pork. Perhaps a few eggs occasionally from the chickens they were not forced to kill, or a few veg-etables from the small garden behind the house.

The chicken leg she stole might have been a large part of the meal, one skinny chicken to feed fourteen or fifteen peo-ple, a feast for Thanksgiving or Christmas or to celebrate her father finding work. Or perhaps the hard times she does not really remember were drawing to a close, and the feast was a sign of better times on the way.

I'm sure she ate the chicken leg. But I like to imagine there was a homeless family nearby that she gave it to, or some-one whose mother or father or great aunt had recently passed away, or one of her younger brothers or sisters who could not stand to wait any longer.

"Here," she says, giving it to them, still dripping gravy. "I only wish there was more."

WEB

My great uncle Paul, after whom I'm named, burned his hands badly a few years before I was born. He drove a propane truck, delivering the volatile gas to old tanks around the countryside, shiny vessels we used to pretend were spacecraft. Climbing on one, you could hear the gas hissing within, and once, when he was clamping the hoses from truck to tank, a stray spark struck and set his hands aflame.

The elder men of my life never spoke of pain, so I imagine him quietly beating out the fire, flailing his hands against his chest, his shirt smoldering, the skin sloughing off, until the fire was finally out. He had several surgeries after the accident, skin grafted from his legs onto his hands, the red fingers turning pink, then finally fading to flesh. The surgeries left him with scars, and the grafts formed webs between each finger.

Something else that happened long before I was born was that he used to get drunk every Saturday night downtown and shoot pool and chase women and finally get carted home by the police. I never knew that part of him, except for how it would swim through me. The man I knew was quiet, with big red hands, a man who mowed paths through the trees and high weeds between our houses so that I might come visit, although I rarely did. As I grew older, I went to see him less and less. Instead, I spent my nights in town, shooting pool and chasing women, drinking too much and occasionally running afoul of the police.

Thirty years after he burned his hands, after the webs formed, when I brought my infant daughter to see him, he could not spread his fingers far enough to play peek-a-boo with her, though he tried. He had grown very old and could hardly hear, but his lined face lit up like fire every time I brought her, and his big hands stretched out to hold her tiny body.

The night his breath blew out for the last time I drank too much at my computer trying to write him back to life. The next morning I woke in pain, the sun coming too strong through the window. I put my hands over my eyes, and saw through the sunlight the thin web of veins in my fingers, the blood beating toward my heart.

LIGHTNING AND
THUNDER

She weighs a hundred pounds shivering wet but calls her biceps Lightning and Thunder. Some days she dresses like a ninja, but in hot pink. Some days I find her so high in the tree in the backyard I can feel where my breath begins and ends, somewhere near the point blood enters and leaves the heart, where the ribcage flutters like the pages of the books she reads while lounging high in the tree, as if this is normal, as if anything our children do is normal.

She tie-dyes her underwear. She wears a shirt with someone else's name on it. She re-upholstered our couch one rainy weekend and now it looks like a dairy cow. When I asked her why, she said she wasn't sure but it seemed like a good idea at the time.

She once told me the War of 1812 started because the British were bamboozling America's trade, so America had to kung fu karate chop them. She once told me George Orwell's real name was Freddy Krueger. I once asked her why she had on two different-colored socks and she replied that she couldn't find the matching one. When I asked her why she didn't simply wear a different pair, she explained that she liked the first sock.

She is fourteen, her shoulders thin and frail as a bird's. Or a kitten, like the one we saw outside the restaurant and she begged to take home. It was in a sorry state—eyes wild as olives, fur matted like my hair in the morning after I fall asleep on the couch. I thought of distemper and rabies and fleas. She thought of clipping out the matted fur, of small bowls of milk on Saturday mornings.

When I found her tie-dyeing her underwear—and socks, and white t-shirts, and one of her first bras, which had the power to make me fear the future and the back seats of cars and frat houses years down the road in some city I've never seen—I asked her why I felt like this was going to cause me trouble. Note that I only meant the mess she might make on the kitchen table, not the fear the cotton and elastic and small hooks stirred in me, but her answer might have been for either thing when she told me that perhaps I needed to do some deep reflecting to find out.

What I reflect on here is her. The mind so like my own, the way the wheels turn when she is thinking, when she stares out the window on October afternoons with the sky so blue it hurts to look at it. Like her eyes. The brown hair. The thin bones that frame her face.

She is the younger of my two daughters. The older one, the first one, we chronicled with pictures and videos, with postcards and finger paintings from preschool. She is the one who tells me, when I say her mother's foot is dirty, to be nice, because I am married to that foot. She is the one who begins sentences with *actually,* or *listen here,* or long dramatic sighs at what she considers my foolishness. She is the one who remembers birthdays and anniversaries, who steals my wife's cell phone and puts hearts and kissy face emojis beside my contact info, who texts me before going to bed when she spends the night with a friend, who sometimes texts me from upstairs to say good night because she doesn't want to walk downstairs.

But not long ago my younger daughter was going through old albums and asked why there weren't any pictures of her. By the time she was born we had gone digital, and most of our pictures of her are stored on the computer, but I suspect we took fewer pictures of our second child, and while she rarely notices the absences in her life, she seemed to take notice of this.

These, then, are excerpts from her life. For those of you who have children, who have made the choice to let your breath walk around outside your body.

Excerpt #1:
During breakfast my wife asks: "What's wrong with the potatoes?"
Daughter the Younger answers: "They're not bacon."

This was last winter, when snow caused the cancellation of school and we stayed home and stood in the kitchen listening to the gas stove tick, our hands held out for warmth, all of us crushed together for the heat of the open oven. I put my arm around my daughters and felt the bones of their shoulders like the hollow wings of birds. Outside it was still snowing. There were downed limbs all over the world and later chainsaws would echo up and down the street. Even looking outside made us cold, so we huddled together for warmth, for the heat of each other's hearts.

We take photos now of everything: our food, our friends, the door of the hotel we stayed in on our way through Tennessee to visit your folks. We take pictures of our new haircuts and our new houses and the spider hanging in the hall closet. We measure out our lives not in coffee spoons but in close-ups, faces reflected in bathroom mirrors early in the morning or late at night, as if we might forget what we look like if not constantly reminded, as if we change so often we have to keep track.

Consider these pictures as well then. Slightly blurry, out of frame. That's my thumb there in the corner. That's my voice telling you to smile. In the frame is my blood, my breath. You'll have to provide your own caption beneath.

Excerpt #2
Me: Why are you spinning?
Daughter the Younger: Why aren't you?

The obvious comparison here is to spin. Me, trying to slow the world, while she wants to speed it up, to become lost, like that game we played as children, dizzying ourselves and trying to walk while everything twists and turns around us, trying to find the righted world. As we grow older we wish for stability. A slowing of movement. A turning back. Watching her spin I feel like I am only trying to find my footing.

But spinning also brings us back to the beginning. To the point the breath begins to draw and the blood begins to burn. Our bodies are made of liquid. We roil within because we are all formed from fluid. To spin is to stir and eventually separate but before that, in each revolution, is a moment of clarity. Here. And here. And here, when we come back to the point where we began. Spinning holds the center in place.

A picture has parameters. It has edges, no matter how far out you pull the focus, how panoramic the view. It has geography: that house, that backyard, that state. That time. When you were pregnant. After she was born but before she was born. You can arrange them in rows, force some semblance of order on them, accord them a position in time, a place.

Not so, memory. Or not always, anyway.

Excerpt #3
Her: I'm going to have some old lady grapes.
Me: Old lady grapes?
Her, as she holds up a box of raisins: Raisins are just old lady grapes.

This excerpt goes with the one before, like a magazine article with the same caption for a series of pictures. The feeling of young and old, of years skipping past until you are as wrinkled as a raisin. But that's not really it, either. It's that the years you want to remember are skipping past and you cannot catch up to them.

It's not that we didn't take any pictures of her. But there seem to be very few of her first years. I am sure they are simply lost somewhere between Arkansas and North Carolina, where we moved when she was a year old. She was teething. A sixteen-hour drive that became a twenty-two-hour drive over three days. There's a picture there as well, one of us pulled over to the side of the interstate to walk a screaming child until she calms while the wind of passing semis rocks the car and the mile markers gleam in the fading sunlight.

We might find them in the hotel room near Fordyce, Arkansas, the one with all the mosquitos, billions of them, so thick they formed a screen in the halo of streetlight in the parking lot where the smell of diesel fuel hung over the stretching rice fields and oil rainbowed in the puddles. Or just outside Knoxville, Tennessee, near where the first hills began to claw their way skyward into the Appalachians and we left our older daughter's doll and she cried most of the way into North Carolina. We do have pictures of our apartment, the one the older daughter skinned her knees running to see, to be the first to enter, while the rest of us hung back, wary of new thresholds. I picked the gravel from her knees while my wife cupped our younger daughter's head, then put her down to crawl on the floor of this new place.

There's a picture there as well, though of course she remembers none of it. When we recount the screaming, the walks along the side of the interstate, the twenty-two-hour drive, she says, "That must have been hard for you," and pats my back as if to comfort me.

I wonder what pictures are comfort, and which confusion. How often we frame ourselves in the best light: a smile, a pose, a peace sign. What is hidden, what stories lie outside the edges.

Excerpt #4
Me: You're small.
Her: I am a ball of fury, and you better be careful.

I wanted her to take karate to learn to defend herself, but what I got were jabs thrown at my head and roundhouses veering toward my groin when I walked past where she was hiding in the hallway. I got joint lock and hip-toss attempts, headlocks, armbars, leg sweeps.

For months I sat on a wooden bench in the dojo in front of a room-length mirror while she punched at men three times her size. She earned her first belt. She said "Yessir" and "Nosir" to the sensei. She bowed at the door to show respect.

When I ask, after another left hook whizzes too close to my eye socket, where her respect for me is, she says, simply, "You're not my sensei," and when I remind her that I have two black belts, and started teaching martial arts when I was her age, she shrugs and says, "I can hit you because you won't hit me back."

Feel free to insert your own images here. A red wagon, a bike with training wheels. Spaghetti in her hair, a birthday cake smeared all over her chubby face. Crying in Santa's lap. Use the old icons. All the archetypes we adhere to. First steps, first words. First breath. Since that's what this is all about anyway.

Excerpt #5
Me: You want to go to a movie with some smelly fourteen-year-old boy?
Her: Would you rather he was nineteen?

I would rather she did not go at all. That she remain. All fathers know this, just as they know that the true value a picture holds is a place in time, one that does not move.

Let us consider now that the lightning could be the flash of the camera. And the thunder comes when you look, years later, at what the lightning captured.

Excerpt #6
Me: Who didn't put the cap back on the toothpaste?
Her: Wasn't me, I haven't brushed today.

Another thing we worry about: teeth. And bones. Skin. Hair. What makes up the heart.

Walking in the park one day she took my arm and started skipping, trying to pull me along. I told her I was too old to be skipping. She said she was too young to not be skipping, which made me think of shuffling cards and flip books. Old movies in which the calendar unfurls to show the passing of time.

Excerpt #7
"The US should just tell the goalie to block everything."

She says this during the World Cup, with a short demonstration that I assume is a goalie blocking everything, but that looks more like a frog hopping side to side. When I laugh at her she punches me in the stomach. I take the punch gracefully, happily. She punches again.

How easy life would be if we could simply block everything that might hurt them. If we could allow them to work out their frustrations on a world that won't hit back.

In raising daughters, sometimes you have to do things you would not normally do. I have worn dresses and high heels and jewelry, have built more forts with Winnie the Pooh pillows and Dora the Explorer bedsheets than I care to count. So much hiding and seeking in the same spots my patience wore as thin as their small shoulders, as the smile I struggled to hold in place.

At the risk of ruining the game forever, here are their favorite hiding spots: behind the couch, under the bed, in the closet. Though you will still spend time looking, even if you have been told exactly where to go and what you will find there.

Some of our older pictures have faded. They have developed sunspots, tiny coronas flaring like the flash of selfies taken in front of the mirror. The color changes, turns sepia, a faded yellow like liver spots, or the light in late afternoon when a storm comes over the hills. You ask when that was. Who those people are. Where is that place.

When we fly back to Arkansas in winter or make the long summer drive through Tennessee, we gather around an old drawer full of photos, passing them from hand to hand. We ask the same old questions, make the same old comments, until we dig down far enough that no one except my grandmother remembers the geography or genealogy, until the pictures are as faded and worn as her hands. Then we all fall silent, pictures fanned around us, occasionally passing one so someone else might see.

Look here, we say. Would you look at that.

As my daughters have grown into teenagers and taken on personalities outside my own, I have been forced to toughen the rules around me. I have banned dramatic sighing in my house, and shoulder shrugs and eye-rolling and sentences that begin with the word "actually." All of my bans work about as well as trying to remember a time before every admonition of mine came with an eye roll or shoulder shrug. About as well as trying to keep them from walking out into a world that may not be kind to them. About as well as the words I whisper when they are crossing the street, or waiting for the bus on a cold January morning while I watch from the window because they are old enough to wait by themselves now, they say.

One evening in the kitchen she dances around me, jabbing at my mid-section. When I tell her she's about to get hurt, she says, "That's an interesting theory," and I think now that this is only theory here, that there is only theory in raising a child. In hoping the world does not hurt them. In hoping you do not hurt them in some way.

In those pictures—the ones we could hold, the finite ones, not the ones stored deep in the machinery of our time—she found one of her. "Here," she said, "here I am," but the photo wasn't of her. Her face fell when her mother told her here, again, was her sister.

Easy to confuse the two, especially in pictures. They stand the same height, now. They have the same eyes, the same color hair. A bit of shade, an off-center flash, can fool the eye into thinking one is the other. I have asked my wife before which one is which. She has hesitated slightly before answering.

As they grow older, they look more like their mother. In younger pictures, they look more like me. Place our pictures side by side to see resemblance. Compare and contrast. My eyes, your nose. When our daughter runs through the house throwing roundhouses at my head, my wife says, "Your daughter." When my daughter rolls her eyes at me I say the same to my wife, as if we are blaming the other for the idiosyncrasies, the slightly off-center craziness of our children. We also claim credit for the good grades, the awards, the athletic achievements, which seems to me, at times, to be a backward way of looking at the world, especially after either one of our daughters has said or done something that I feel compelled to write down, to keep as a record. Like a picture. One we frame and place on the mantel, right next to the Christmas photos.

Sight itself is circular. Messages pass from the eye to the brain and back. Light waves travel from distant objects to form images in our eyes, which are translated by the brain. What we see is not really what we see, only an interpretation. What a father sees when he looks at his daughter is different from what the world sees. What you see in these excerpts will be different from my intent. Meaning is lost in the circuitous route from the page to your brain and back again. From my brain to my fingers to the screen.

Pictures are no better. I can show you, for example, one from her third grade year, but it doesn't show the days she came home crying because the other kids made fun of her slight speech impediment. Or how she stayed up so late at night sounding out her S's in front of a mirror that she fell asleep waiting for the bus the next morning. How she didn't talk all the next day, and the day after that, for fear of how her words might be heard. You will not know how I also stayed up late, drinking so much that my angry words were slurred worse than hers had ever been.

For a story like this we need words, even knowing they will fail. Take the slur of the S. From there say *sleep* and *speech* and *sorrow*. Those will get you closer than any picture ever could, though we always fall short.

At age four she fell down the second-floor stairs, flipping head over heels, her thin bones striking the hard wooden steps. At ages eight and five both our daughters were lost among the big buildings downtown when a parade float driver failed to return them to the appropriate parking lot, dropped them off in a back alley, and every backfire or raised voice we heard for the forty-five minutes it took to find them sounded like the collapse of stars.

At eighteen months the doctors feared our older daughter's head was misaligned. My wife came home crying fiercely from a routine doctor's visit. Our daughter's brain could be squeezed as her skull hardened. As nurses slid her into an MRI machine a week later, I felt like my heart was being squeezed together as hard as my wife dug her fingernails into my arm.

The MRI took pictures of her skull. Not that different from an ultrasound taking pictures inside the womb. We prop photos beside the casket so that our lives begin and end with pictures, but that day we only cared what the MRI did not show. I don't need a picture for that. Only this: we waited in a little room until our daughter woke up. The passing feet of nurses went past and machines beeped and clicked and at some point the doctor came to tell us the scan showed nothing abnormal, that everything was fine. He pointed to a picture to illustrate his point.

My maternal grandmother lost an infant sister during the Great Depression. My paternal grandmother lost her first child. My stepsister lost her eighteen-month-old son. We have pictures of them somewhere, but no words. No deeds. We fall silent looking into those places inside us where we carry the pictures we remember.

But finally here's the hospital photo, the one with a blank space for a name, a weight, which we later fill in and file away and occasionally take out and hold to the light and wonder at the time that has passed between then and now, compare what we hold in our hands with what we hold in our hearts. Like lessons, or lightning. Like thought and thunder.

Because you can't know, on that day you bring her home from the hospital, what pictures and personalities will be formed. What geography lies ahead. You have only the ultra-sound to go on, and then the birth picture, which you forget to look at until she no longer looks that way, because you have her now. These new lungs, this new breath.

HIDE-AND-SEEK

The story—and it's an old one—goes like this: my mother went inside for half a second, and my brother and I disappeared. One minute we were there, and then we were not. She looked in the garage and behind the barn. She checked to make sure the iron cover was over the old well. She searched for almost an hour, or whatever passes for an hour in a mother's mind when her children are missing, and was on the edge of calling the cops or just crying uncontrollably, when she heard us laughing.

My brother and I were three and four at the time and only wanted, we told her, to play hide-and-seek. We had crouched down behind the holly bushes that grew so close together only someone our size could see how to get in, and ignored her repeated calls. I have no memory of any of this, but we must have found it funny to see her frantically searching. When she found us, she says, there was quite a spanking, though only after she'd hugged us hard enough to hurt.

The story, for my mother, is one of fear. For my brother and me a remembering, not of the hiding, but of the old house and the holly bushes. Of cold winter mornings before the fireplace got going, and warm summer nights when the fireflies were hitting in the fields in front of our house.

For my first daughter, who has loved hearing the story since before she was old enough to understand it, it is something else. She laughs so hard when my mother tells it she can't quite breathe, blue eyes tearing at the corners. I'd say she finds it funny that her father and favorite uncle got a spanking, that her Nana was frantic, that it became something to laugh about years later.

She must also remember hiding from me when she was a child. When I think of hide-and-seek, I rarely remember the summer nights of my childhood, silent among the peach trees in the last light while cousins searched for me, no sense of time but the moon coming up or our mothers calling us, but of her asking to play every afternoon.

We had just moved to North Carolina then, and lived in a small apartment. I had just started graduate school. I wrote in the mornings, then picked up my daughters, ages one and four, from daycare at noon. Some days we went to the park and some days we walked across campus to the library, but most days, for at least an hour or what seemed an eternity, we hid from each other.

She always insisted I count to a hundred. I could never bring myself to tell her there were only a few places to hide in our apartment, and no matter if I counted to a million all I had to do was search them in order: behind the couch, behind the bed, behind the bathroom door.

I also did not tell her that when I yelled "Ready or not here I come" she should not answer with "Okay, Daddy!" I suppose someone might say I was cheating, but I found it charming. She wasn't yet old enough to know I could track her by her voice, or maybe she only wanted to always answer me. At that age I suppose it didn't occur to her not to answer.

So I'd count, carrying my younger daughter with me, then call out and hear her answer. For fun I'd look in the few other places first before finding her and pretending to be surprised. She'd be crouched down behind the couch, trying not to laugh, blue eyes the same color as my own looking up at me. My younger daughter would tap her sister on the shoulder as if to claim her found. Then it was my turn, and I'd hear her counting while I'd hide with my younger daughter, who was not quite old enough to know what was going on but old enough to find it fun. We would slip behind the bathroom door or lie beneath the bed or stand in the shower with the curtain pulled and try not to laugh when she came creeping in. I'm still surprised how hard it was not to laugh, how difficult to keep quiet when I saw the look of concentration on her face.

Then she'd find me and I'd be forced to count again, and I admit, because I'm trying to be honest here, that some days I did not want to play. There were too many things to do or I was too tired. Sometimes I only pretended to count while I closed my eyes for a few moments of rest, and sometimes I fell asleep while waiting for her to find me. Our younger daughter did not sleep through every night and sometimes I stayed up late at my computer, trying to write the world or at least make my family a better place in it. It seems I was always too tired to pay much attention to what mattered, but what I hope my daughter thinks when she hears the story about my brother and me hunkered down behind the holly, our mother frantically searching, is that what we really have, what we'll try to hold onto later, is often hidden from us.

THIS ONE
WILL HURT YOU

Brian's on his front porch when I get there, leaned back in a two-dollar lawn chair, a beer resting on his stomach and his vaguely western shirt unbuttoned halfway. There's a splotch of paint on his shorts. His fingernails are dirty. There are trimmed limbs down in the yard, and the air smells of cut grass.

He hands me a beer as I walk up on the porch. His dog sits up and wags its tail. It's early on a Sunday afternoon in October, and the day has warmed. The leaves are just changing colors on the trees, and the nights are cool. Lawn mowers rattle up and down the street. We stand on the porch in the warm afternoon and smoke and drink, waving at the neighbors out for a walk. Brian's dog shuffles between our feet. He barks at a man passing on the sidewalk.

By the time Quinn arrives, we are deep into our second beers. The afternoon football games have started on TV, and we alternate between the porch and the living room, coming out to smoke, cursing the players on the opposing team during time-outs and commercials. Brian tells us those sons of bitches couldn't play for his junior high team. He says they all ought to be shot for such poor play.

The dog wanders off during one of the front porch smokes, and we circle the block until we find him. It is not a great neighborhood. Brian's end of the street is fine, but not far down, the empty lots and sagging houses begin. One of the houses sells crack, we are sure. The three men who live there sit on the porch much like we are doing, but cars pull in and out all afternoon. A woman parks, gets out on shaking heels, climbs the steps. One of the men holds the door for her. Ten minutes later she comes out and drives away.

Inside, our team is losing, or winning, it doesn't really matter, but it seems to matter then, before the kitten. The windows are open and the warm day comes in, the curtains sucked in and out by the slight breeze. A last few bumblebees buzz around the newly trimmed shrubs that flank Brian's house. The air smells of honeysuckle.

The dog whines at the back door. Brian has had the dog for longer than I've known him, though for the first two years of their relationship, the dog never came close enough for Brian to touch. He ate the food Brian put out and slept under the porch and ran away when anyone approached. He was half wild, almost feral.

When we go back out on the porch a few leaves are falling from the trees. We turn up our beers. The sky is so blue it hurts somewhere inside. The sun is shifting slowly toward the west now, and I think that when the shadows start to run together we will regret the end of this day. There is work tomorrow, responsibilities, and when it gets full dark and the stars begin to come out and the air turns cold enough that we can measure our breaths before us, we will wonder why all good things must come to an end. We will think of all the time we have wasted, the savings accounts we haven't yet started, the family members we haven't visited in years.

Halftime of the game we head for the backyard to throw the football around. Brian's dog chases it from person to person. If anyone drops it he tries to get it, and we have to fight him off. He thinks it a great fun game. After a couple of years the dog began to follow Brian when he went for walks through

the woods. He'd chase squirrels and rabbits, would seize wood-
chucks along the banks of creeks and shake them to death.
Gradually, he domesticated. Brian let him inside the house.

Our team completely loses it in the second half, and we
curse and scream at them. Their bad play chases us to the front
porch again. One night last summer we heard shouting from
across the street and came out to watch a man and woman
standing in their front yard cursing one another. The woman
threw armloads of clothes out the front door while the man
threatened to strike her. The man was drunk. The woman
drunker. The fight meandered over the yard until the man
finally climbed in his car. The woman tried to block him. When
he got past her he roared around the neighborhood until the
cops caught him.

As we stand on the porch there seems to be something waiting for us, some thing hovering in the air that we can't quite
define. It might be the work none of us want to go to in the
morning. It might be that we just don't want the day to end, the
long Sundays of fall when we have nothing to do, no responsibilities to wives or families, only men gathering to drink and
burp and curse one another in jest. Another woman pulls in at
the crack dealer's house and another man goes inside with her
and we know she is most likely going down on him for crack.
Brian declares the entire football season a loss, then ignores
me when I wonder aloud why we get so upset over two teams
trying to control the space of a hundred yards. We smoke and
stare at the sun settling in the turned leaves, lighting them like
fire.

At the end of the game Brian throws up his hands. His dog
begins to bark at the back door. We do not see the little kitten
stealthily crossing the backyard, but the dog does. He shoots
out the door like a rifle when I open it. Brian yells for him to
stop, but he does not stop.

By the time we pull the dog off, the kitten's back is broken.
Its eyes are wide, full black. It is bleeding from the dog's teeth,
the white fur turning pink. Its front paws claw at the ground
but its back legs don't move so it only spins in a circle, hissing

at us in fear. Brian takes the dog inside. It barks at us from the back door, its legs splayed against the screen.

We stand looking down at the kitten. We look at one another. Brian says *Goddammit* very softly. The sun sits just above the house and our shadows stretch long. I reach down to pet the kitten but it hisses at me, spinning, trying to get away. I can tell it is terrified, and confused. For the next few months I will replay the scene in my head again and again: the dog shooting out the back door, none of us quick enough to realize what he is doing. The pounce onto the little white blur, the quick shake of the head that snaps its back.

The kitten is white with a few black spots. I kneel down beside it and look up at Brian and Quinn. A few years ago we went to grad school together to learn to write, and what we came up with were stories about women we'd slept with and fistfights we'd won, the false romantic notion all too often portrayed in male fiction, the Hemingway-esque idea of tough drink and tougher fists, of man embracing his animal nature, his darkness and depravity. When the kitten looks up at me, I realize we had no idea what we were writing about, not a fucking clue.

Beside me, Brian says *Goddammit* again. Quinn says, also very softly, as if he doesn't want to scare the kitten, that its back is broken. I want to tell Quinn *No fucking shit, Sherlock,* or something just as cutting and condescending because it is obvious the kitten's back is broken—quick head shake, snap—but I don't. I realize Quinn needed to say something. I realize I need to say something but I don't know what it would be.

The dog is still barking at the back door. Another lawn mower fires up on an adjacent street. My shadow looms large and distorted on the lawn. There is an empty lot past Brian's fence, and I find myself wondering why the damn kitten didn't use the empty lot, why it had to come into Brian's yard. I wonder who its owners are and curse them for not taking better care of it, but I only do all this because I do not want to look at the kitten or think about the thing that is right in front of us. I want the sun to go down and the day to be over. I want darkness to fall and to be sober, to be in bed with my wife or reading to my children upstairs.

Brian goes back inside to shut the dog up. I hear him telling the dog he is an asshole. Quinn says, *I can't look at this,* and goes inside. The cat opens its mouth when I try to pet it, but no sound comes out. The dirt is scuffed in a circle where it has been trying to get up and walk. The blood is already drying in its fur, matting it together. Leaves and dirt stick to the blood. Its sides heave in and out. It no longer tries to spin.

I yell for Brian to bring me a beer. I don't want to leave the cat. What I mean is, I absolutely want to leave the cat. I want to run down the street to home, or to the crack dealer's house, or the house of the guy who yells at his wife while she heaves his laundry into the front yard. What I mean is: I don't want to be here, watching the cat die. What I mean is: I don't want to be here, hoping that it dies soon.

Brian brings me a beer. My pleasant October buzz is gone. The lawn mowers are too loud. I look at Brian and Quinn. We discuss options without saying real words, skirting the issue we know is in front of us. All our options circle around one thing: its back is broken. We could call a veterinarian, but its back is broken. We could call a nurse Brian knows, but its back is broken.

There's not a damn thing you can do for a broken back, Brian says, which is what we've all been thinking: There's not a damn thing you can do.

Quinn has stopped drinking. I feel sick. The grass in the empty lot is too high. We hear a siren somewhere across town. There is a terrible thing about the October light in the late afternoon. Even the kitten throws a shadow. Brian says, *Everything that ever happened happened in October,* and I think he is drunk until I realize he is quoting one of his own lines from a long-ago story. It seems as if we are reading an old story, only we know how this story ends. There's a climax, then an unknotting that reveals the true meaning of everything. Or maybe we don't know how this will end at all.

The kitten has managed to crawl under an old board a few feet away, dragging its lower body behind it. We hear it meow once, a cry like a newborn in the night. Quinn says *I can't,* but doesn't tell us what he can't do.

Brian goes in for water. Quinn won't look at the cat. The dog is still barking. The air feels too warm now, though it is growing colder. My mouth tastes like bile, but I keep drinking.

Brian comes out carrying the water dish carefully and places it beside the cat. The bowl is too high for the cat to reach so he goes inside for a saucer. The kitten scoots away as he sets it down. He pushes it closer. The kitten's pink tongue laps delicately at the water. It closes its eyes for a moment.

We step back a few paces so the kitten won't hear what we are saying. We wonder where we can get a veterinarian at six o'clock on a Sunday evening. We wonder what the fuck he could do.

This leaves us standing in the backyard not looking at one another while the shadows stitch themselves together. Quinn suggests we wait. He says the kitten could only spin in a circle at first and then after only a little while crawled under the board. He says the kitten began to lap at the water. Brian goes in for food. He opens a can of tuna and places it beside the water saucer. We decide to wait and see.

We go onto the front porch. More cars pull in and out at the crack dealer's house. We are certain the men deal crack. We are certain now, in this mood, that the three men have guns and hand grenades. We are certain the man who yelled at his wife is wanted in five states. We are certain the wife is wanted as well. We take turns wandering to the back of the house to peer out the window. We say things like *It might have moved a little* and *I think it ate some tuna.* We splash water on our faces at the sink. We drink more beer, but it doesn't help. Brian turns the music off—it doesn't seem right to have it on. I nod my head at him as if he has done something noble.

When we go into the backyard again the kitten hasn't moved. It hasn't gotten better. It's not going to get better. Its sides still heave. The blood is dried dark on its fur. It hisses when I try to pet it. The grass is too high in the empty yard. The light is terrible. Brian says *Goddammit* again. Quinn says *We should wait*, but we all know there is nothing to wait for, and no reason. We can see the pain in its milky eyes.

Which leaves us standing in a circle looking at one another. Things pass between us unsaid. I won't explain what they are. You should understand by now where this is going.

Brian says, *I can't. I can't fucking do it. Not in any way. Not happening.* Quinn shakes his head. He walks a few steps away and then walks back, still shaking his head. He raises his hand and lets it fall. *No,* he says. *Not ever. I can't,* and this time we all know what he can't do.

And now you listen to me, because I want you to know what I did, what I think about sometimes late at night in a quiet house when everyone else is asleep. The thing's back was broken, its eyes like clouds on a backdrop of blue sky. One paw twitched. It shook its head to keep the flies away. It lay bleeding into the dirt, and though I knew my suffering would last longer, I did not think it would be as much. I remember now the quality of the light. I remember thinking of my daughters. I remember thinking I am about to kill this thing, all thoughts as distant as the wind, the terrible sun starting down, ending this fine day in October, when everything that ever happens happens.

Brian and Quinn went inside. I stood looking down at the kitten for a while. I might have said something to it, offered some words of comfort or farewell. After a time I adjusted the board to where it covered the kitten's little head. It meowed from under the board, a low whine of fear. I told it *Hush now, hush.* Then I brought my heel down on the board hard and quick and I want to say I heard another snapping sound but I do not trust this memory any more than the earlier one, less so for I was having trouble seeing with my suddenly doubled vision and trouble hearing with the whine and cry and shatter that ran through my head, the sound of things breaking, not all of them on the outside. I stomped on the board again, wanting it to be over, making sure it was. My eyes were hot.

A hard cold lump had formed in my stomach. I walked to the fence and leaned over and vomited, trying to get everything out of me.

Brian and Quinn ignored my red eyes. Brian put a hand on my shoulder. He said something, words. Quinn did too. I don't remember what they were. I doubt they meant anything. Brian got a shovel from the shed and we dug a hole at the far back of his yard and put the kitten in the hole and covered it. Its eyes were still open: none of us had the strength to close them.

I don't remember if we said any words or not. I doubt they would have meant anything. We are shameful creatures, scared of death, so we hurried back to sit in the front room without looking at one another as the afternoon passed into evening. After a time Brian got up and went to the refrigerator and grabbed three beers and passed them around. We stood in the gathering darkness and drank, trying to forget, which I can tell you for sure never works.

ACKNOWLEDGMENTS

Writing does not happen in a vacuum, I seem to recall some one saying once, and so it is. As much time as I spent alone at my computer writing this book, it never would have gotten out of that room without the help of many, many people.

Thanks to the editors of literary journals who first published these essays: Roxane Gay, Amy Wright, Dan Latimer, Matthew Olzmann, Willard Spiegelman, Sheryl Monk, Beth Blachman, Terry Kennedy, Soma Mei Sheng Frazier, Sally Molini, Karen Rigby, Fiona Sze-Lorrain, and Ben George. Special thanks also to Robert Atwan of the Best American Essays series for reprinting "Storm Country" (2005) and "After the Ice" (2011). These essays previously appeared in the following journals:

"After the Ice," *Southern Humanities Review*
"My Possum Problem, and How it Finally Ended," *Cerise Press*
"The Wild Thing With People Feet Was My Favorite," *The Rumpus*
"The Night Before Christmas," *Cerise Press*
"Cold," *Southwest Review*

"Of Little Faith," *StorySouth*
"Storm Country," *Southern Humanities Review*
"Girl on the Third Floor," *Ecotone*
"The Bear," *Slice*
"Palm Sunday," *COG*
"Brief and Selected History," *Diagram*
"The Giving of Food," *Southwest Review*
"Web," *Change Seven*
"Lightning and Thunder," *Zone 3*
"This One Will Hurt You," *The Collagist*

Thanks to the fine people at The Ohio State University Press: David Lazar, Patrick Madden, and Kristen Elias Rowley, not only for giving this collection a home, but for acknowledging the essay, a form that seeks answers when so much of the world does not.

Fred Chappell, Michael Parker, and Lee Zacharias at the University of North Carolina at Greensboro deserve my respect and admiration, as does the inestimable Jim Clark, may he rest in peace. Thanks to my workshop mates MC Armstrong, JT Hill, David Bowen, and Jenny Noller Johnson—I could not have written better friends into being. Thanks to Brian Crocker, editor and Radio Room operator extraordinaire, who never shied away from telling me when an essay was terrible, and to Okla Elliott, King of the Porch, who left us too soon.

Thanks to Michael Karl Ritchie for telling me to never give up, and Carl Brucker for his rendition of "Tyger, Tyger" on electric guitar.

Much appreciation to Michael Gills, for teaching me that writing is not something one simply does, but is a way of being. That writing is a habit, that words matter, that work matters—I'm forever grateful for these lessons.

This book is about, at its heart, family, the storytellers who shaped me into what am I today: my mother, who read to me until her voice grew hoarse; my brother, who taught me to shape sentences; my father and stepfather and grandfathers, whose stories were woods and wind, the careful observation of the landscape we live in; my grandmothers who told their own stories, often in silence. I hope they will all take the words here as partial payment for a debt I can never erase.

Last but not least, thanks to Lisa, for being such a kind and caring partner, for putting up with all my hiding away so could I write these words. And for Haley and Savannah, my wild things, my stars, my lightning strikes.

21st CENTURY ESSAYS
David Lazar and Patrick Madden, Series Editors

This series from Mad Creek Books is a vehicle to discover, publish, and promote some of the most daring, ingenious, and artistic nonfiction. This is the first and only major series that announces its focus on the essay—a genre whose plasticity, timelessness, popularity, and centrality to nonfiction writing make it especially important in the field of nonfiction literature. In addition to publishing the most interesting and innovative books of essays by American writers, the series publishes extraordinary international essayists and reprint works by neglected or forgotten essayists, voices that deserve to be heard, revived, and reprised. The series is a major addition to the possibilities of contemporary literary nonfiction, focusing on that central, frequently chimerical, and invariably supple form: The Essay.